15 Vulg
19 Appea
21 Mask

100 BEST QUOTES
OF NICCOLO MACHIAVELLI

23 Putin

24 Appearances not reality
25 No oppression
26 War
27 Act not repent

Introduction

Niccolo Machiavelli (1469-1527) was an Italian political philosopher, diplomat, and writer, best known for his influential work "The Prince" (Il Principe), written in 1513. Machiavelli lived during the Renaissance era and is considered one of its key figures.

In his book "The Prince," Machiavelli explored the nature of political power and the strategies of governance. He presented his vision of a wise and strong ruler who could make tough decisions in the interest of the state, even if it required ruthlessness and unpopular actions. The book became renowned for its controversial ideas, such as "the end justifies the means" and how rulers must balance morality with political reality.

> Everyone sees what you appear to be, few experience what you really are.

> If an injury has to be done to a man it should be so severe that his vengeance need not be feared.

> The first method for estimating the intelligence of a ruler is to look at the men he has around him.

> There is no other way to guard yourself against flattery than by making men understand that telling you the truth will not offend you.

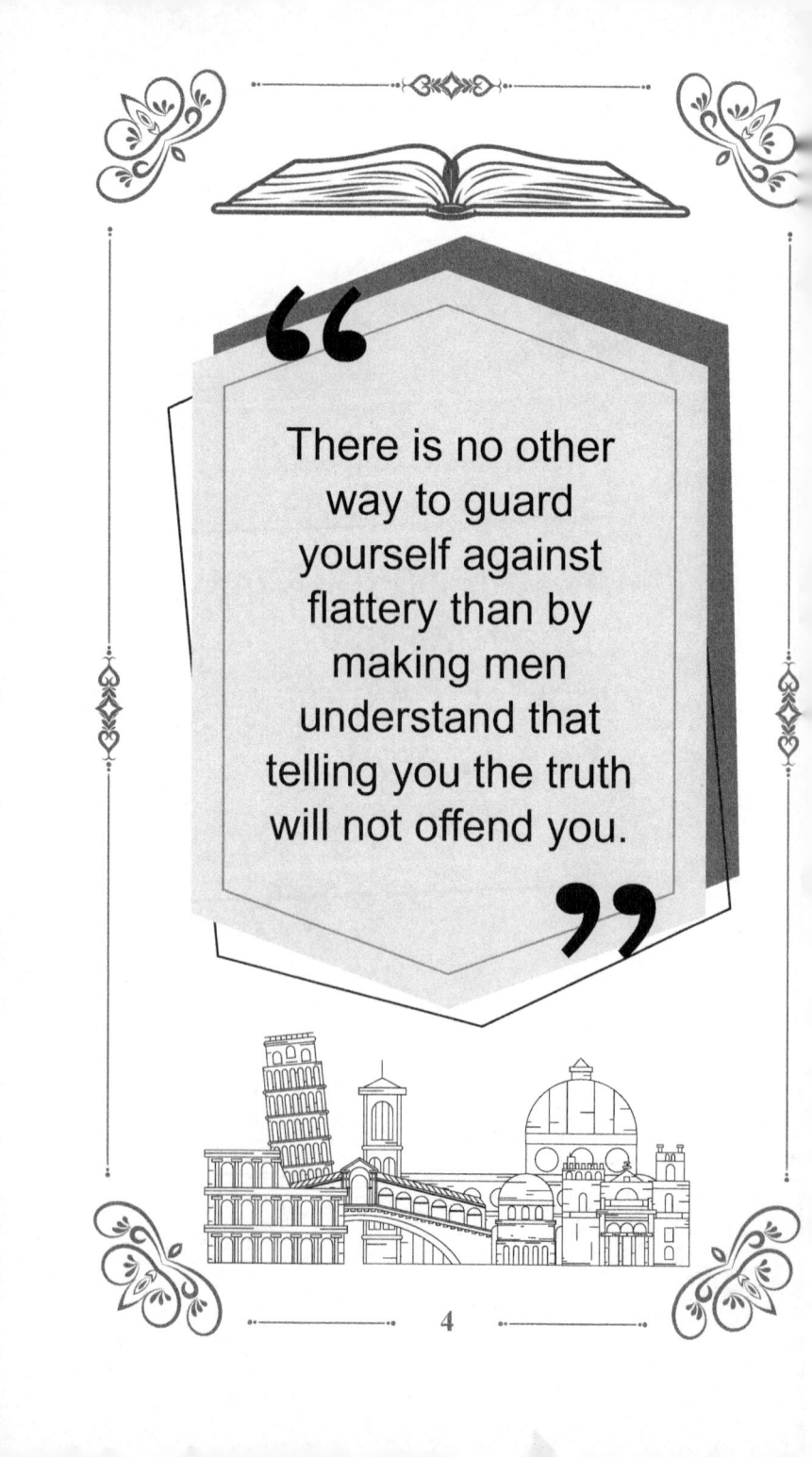

> The lion cannot protect himself from traps, and the fox cannot defend himself from wolves. One must therefore be a fox to recognize traps, and a lion to frighten wolves.

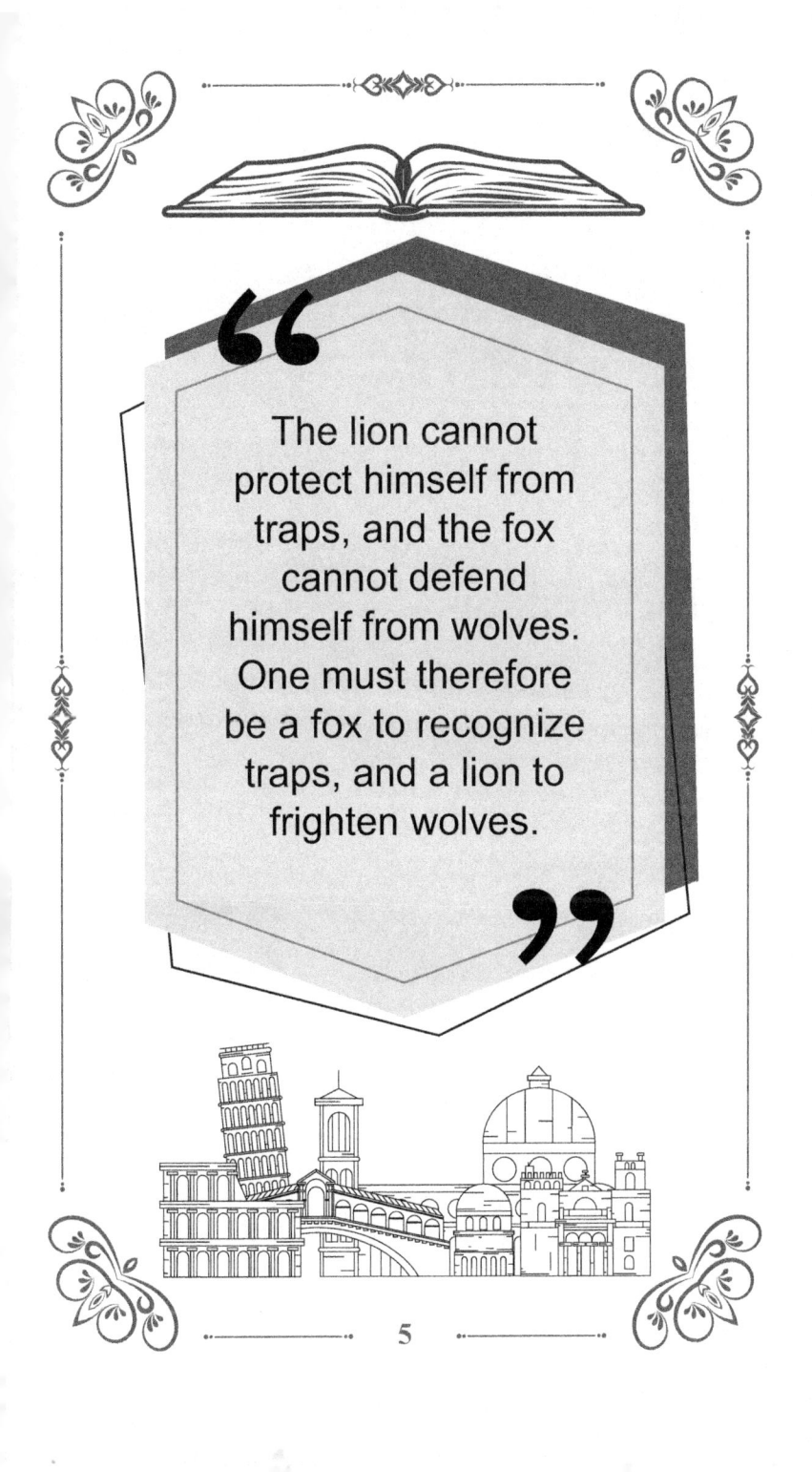

> Never was anything great achieved without danger.

> It is much safer to be feared than loved because love is preserved by the link of obligation which, owing to the baseness of men, is broken at every opportunity for their advantage; but fear preserves you by a dread of punishment which never fails.

> Never attempt to win by force what can be won by deception.

> All courses of action are risky, so prudence is not in avoiding danger (it's impossible), but calculating risk and acting decisively. Make mistakes of ambition and not mistakes of sloth. Develop the strength to do bold things, not the strength to suffer.

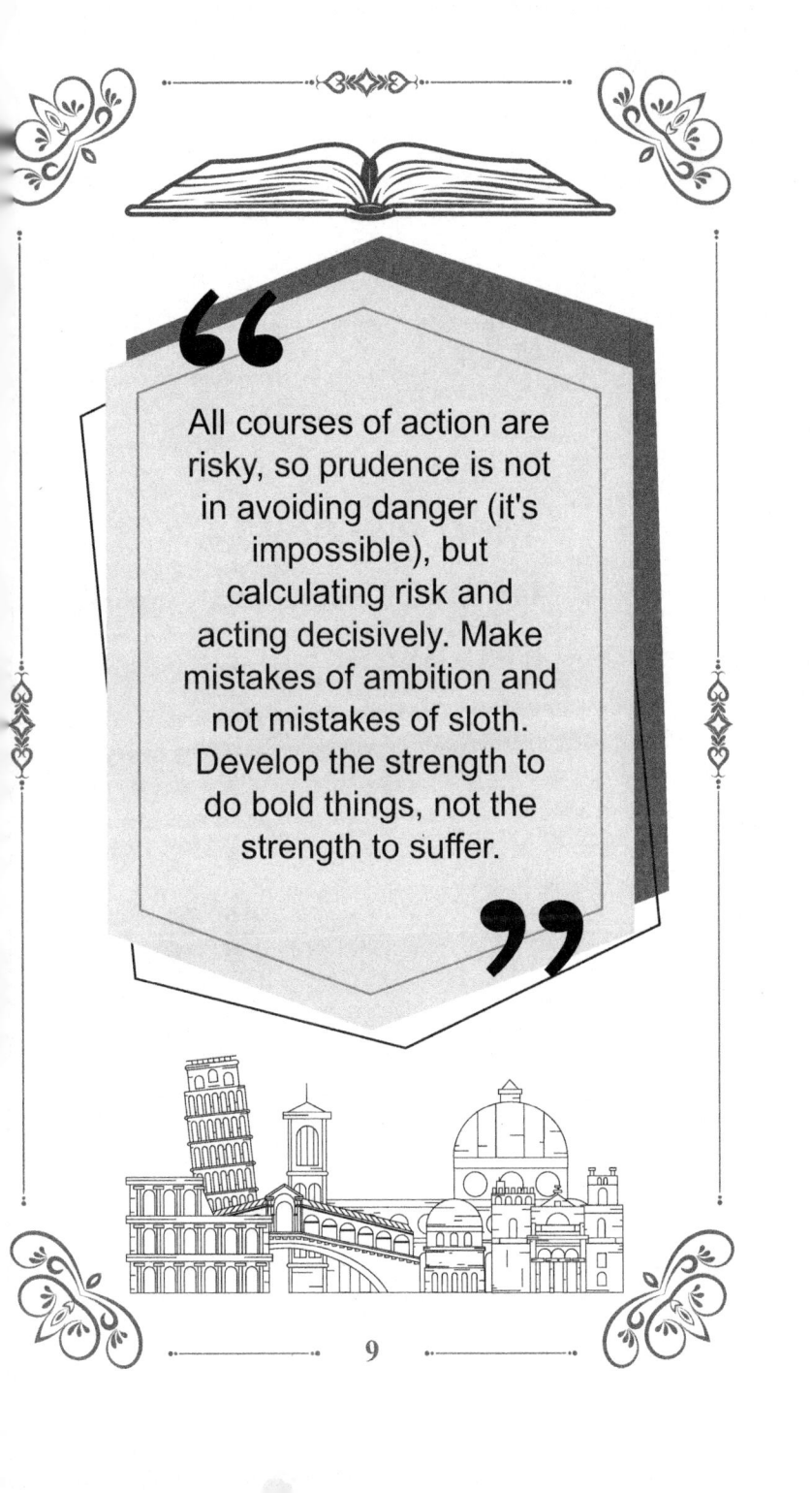

> Men are driven by two principal impulses, either by love or by fear.

> There are three classes of intellects: one which comprehends by itself; another which appreciates what others comprehend; and a third which neither comprehends by itself nor by the showing of others; the first is the most excellent, the second is good, the third is useless.

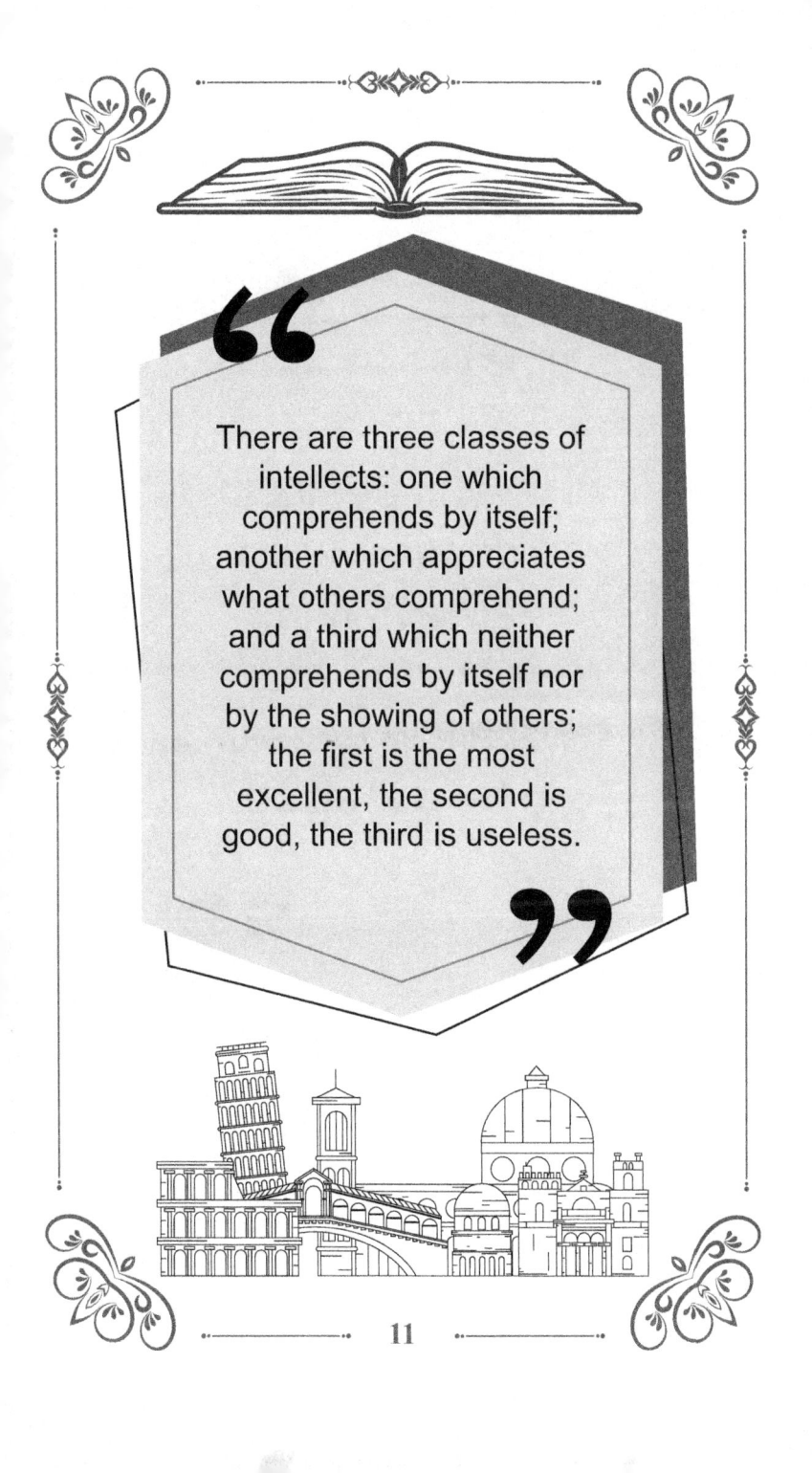

> He who seeks to deceive will always find someone who will allow himself to be deceived.

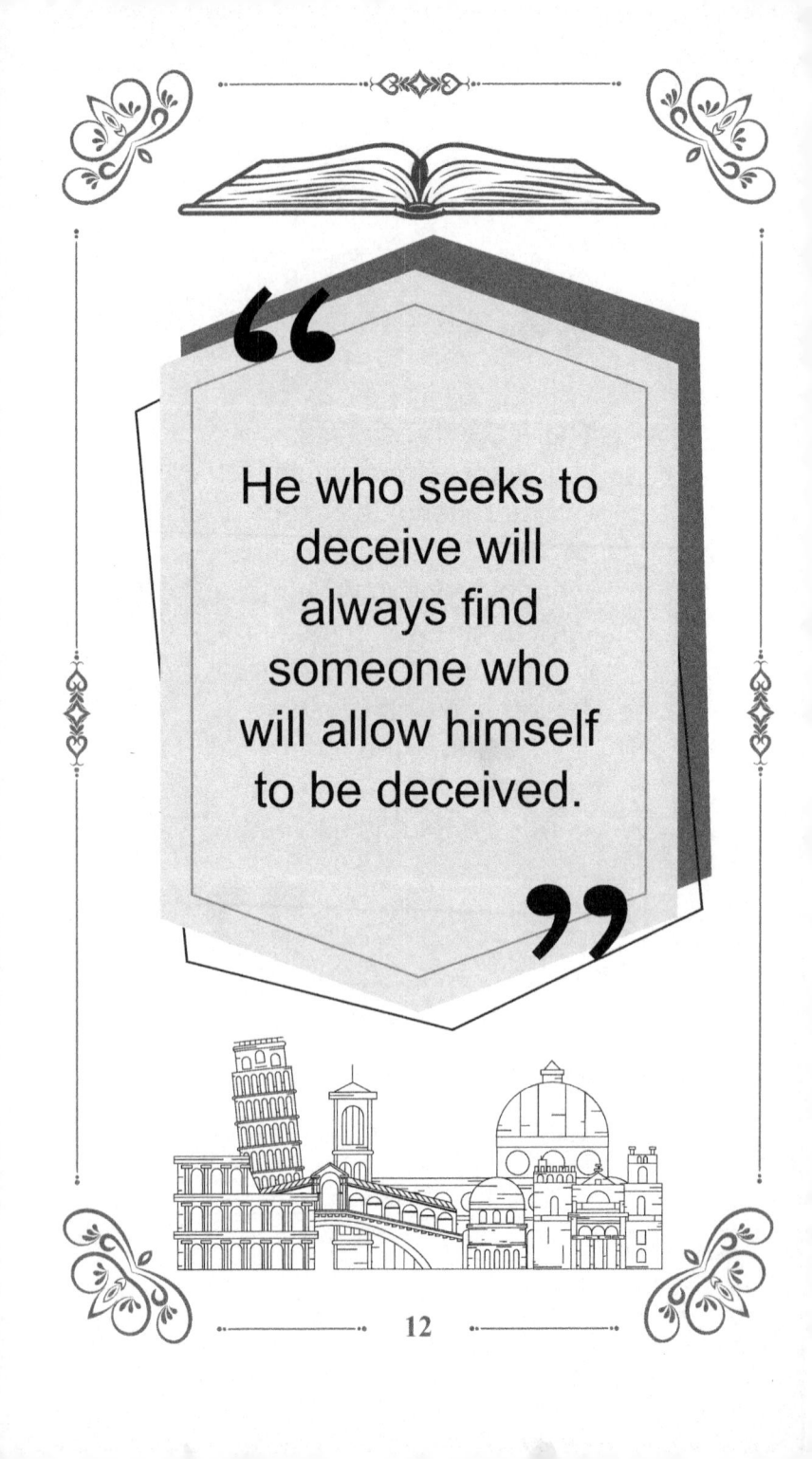

> How we live is so different from how we ought to live that he who studies what ought to be done rather than what is done will learn the way to his downfall rather than to his preservation.

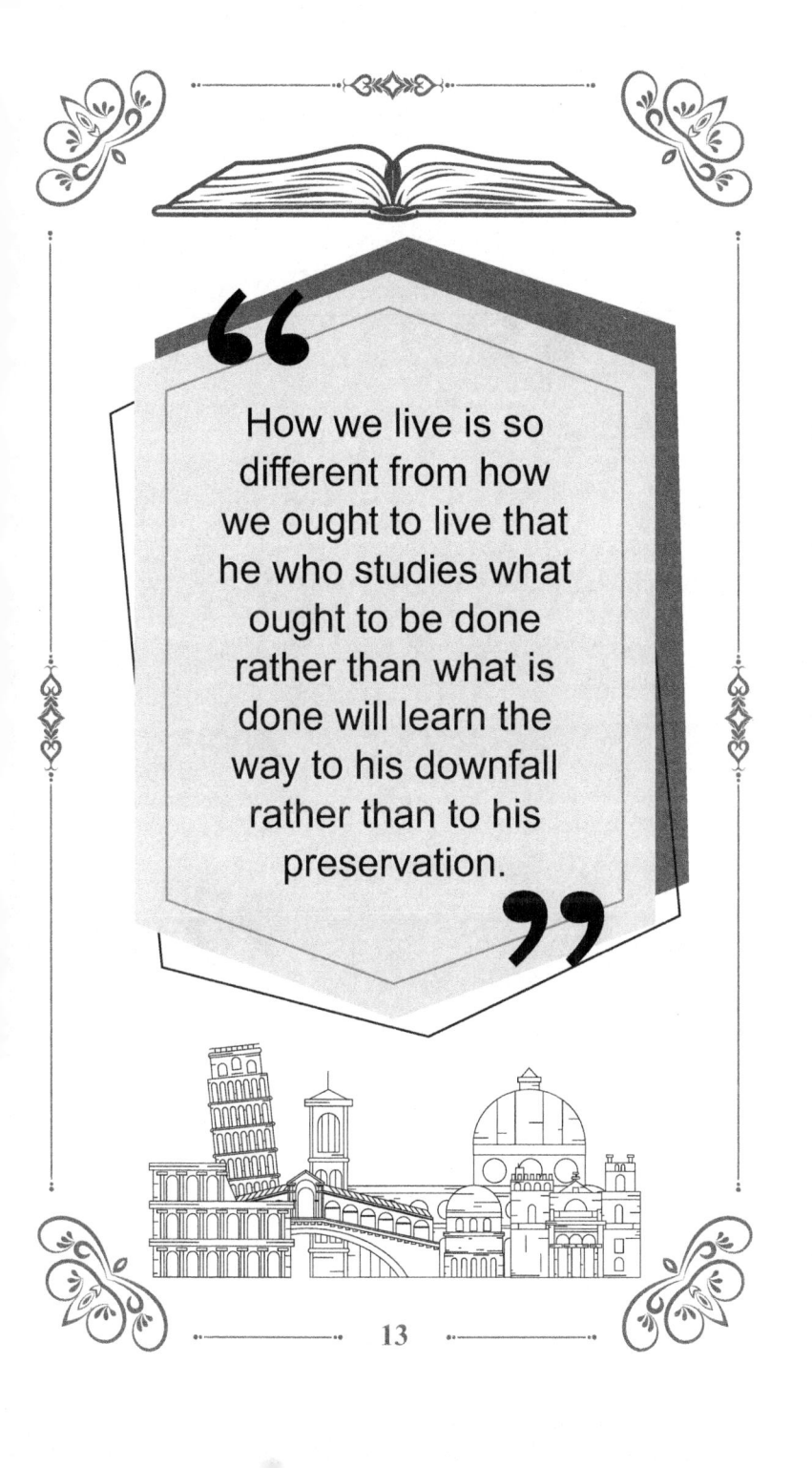

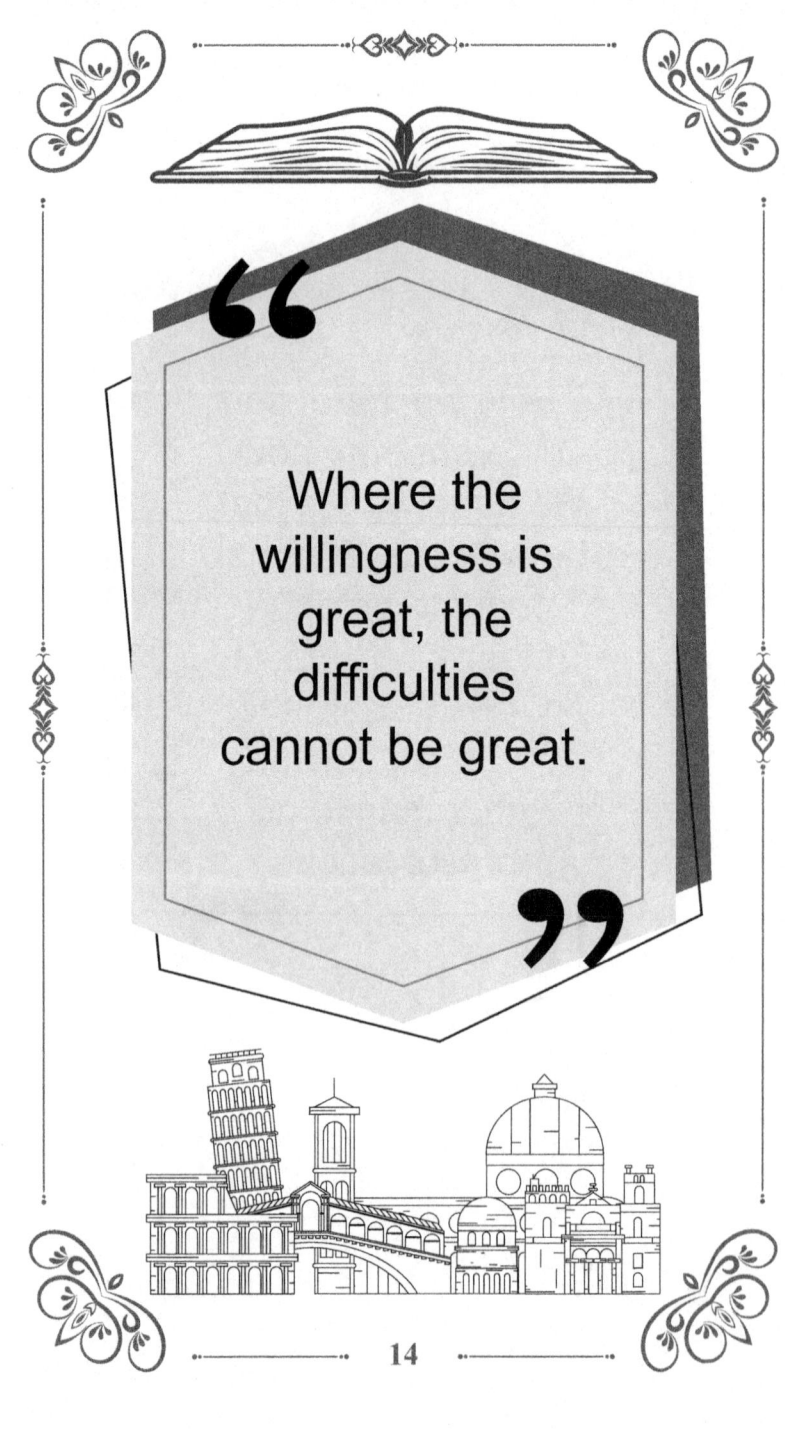

> Where the willingness is great, the difficulties cannot be great.

> The vulgar crowd always is taken by appearances, and the world consists chiefly of the vulgar.

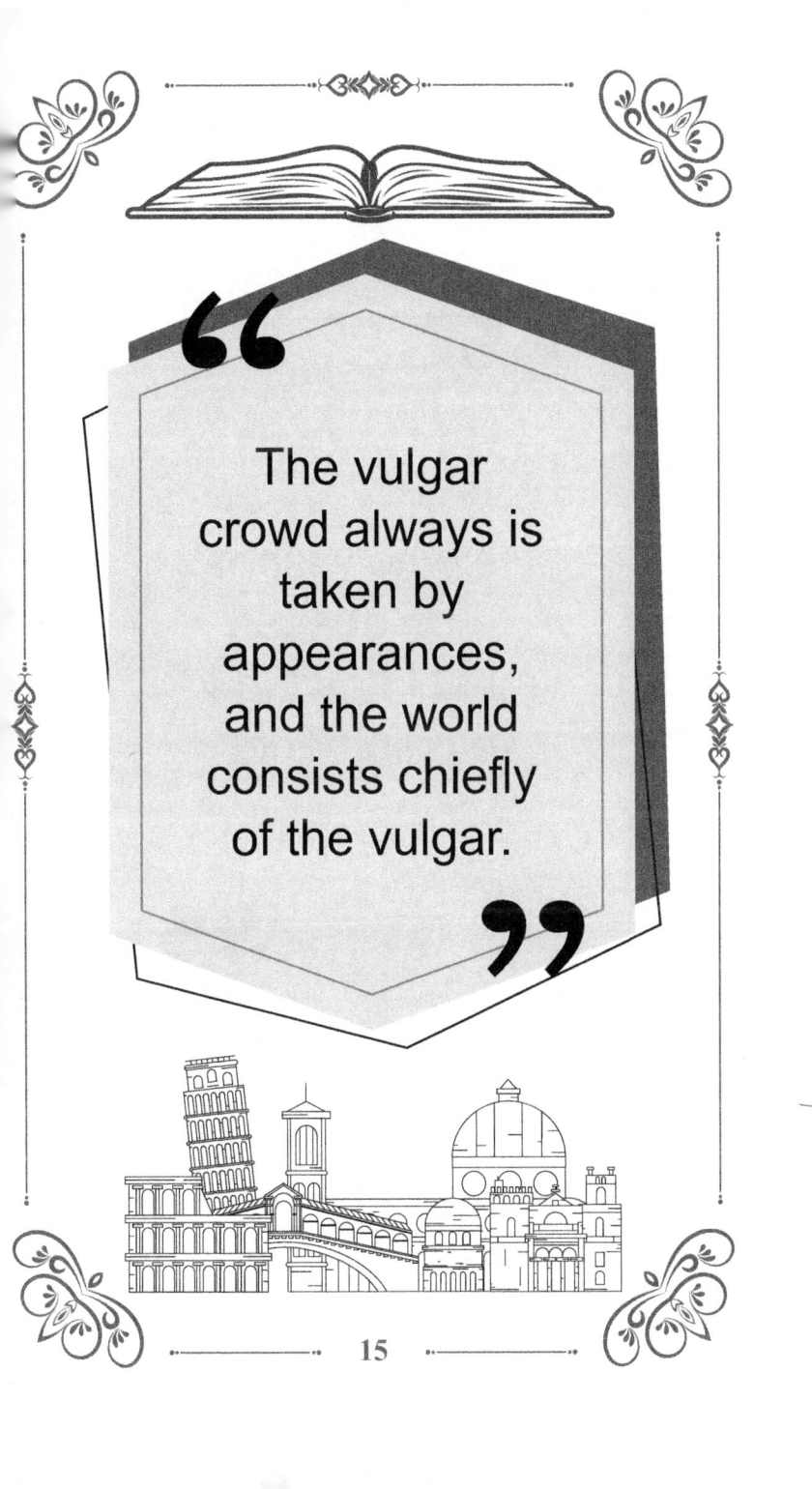

> He who wishes to be obeyed must know how to command.

> A man who is used to acting in one way never changes; he must come to ruin when the times, in changing, no longer are in harmony with his ways.

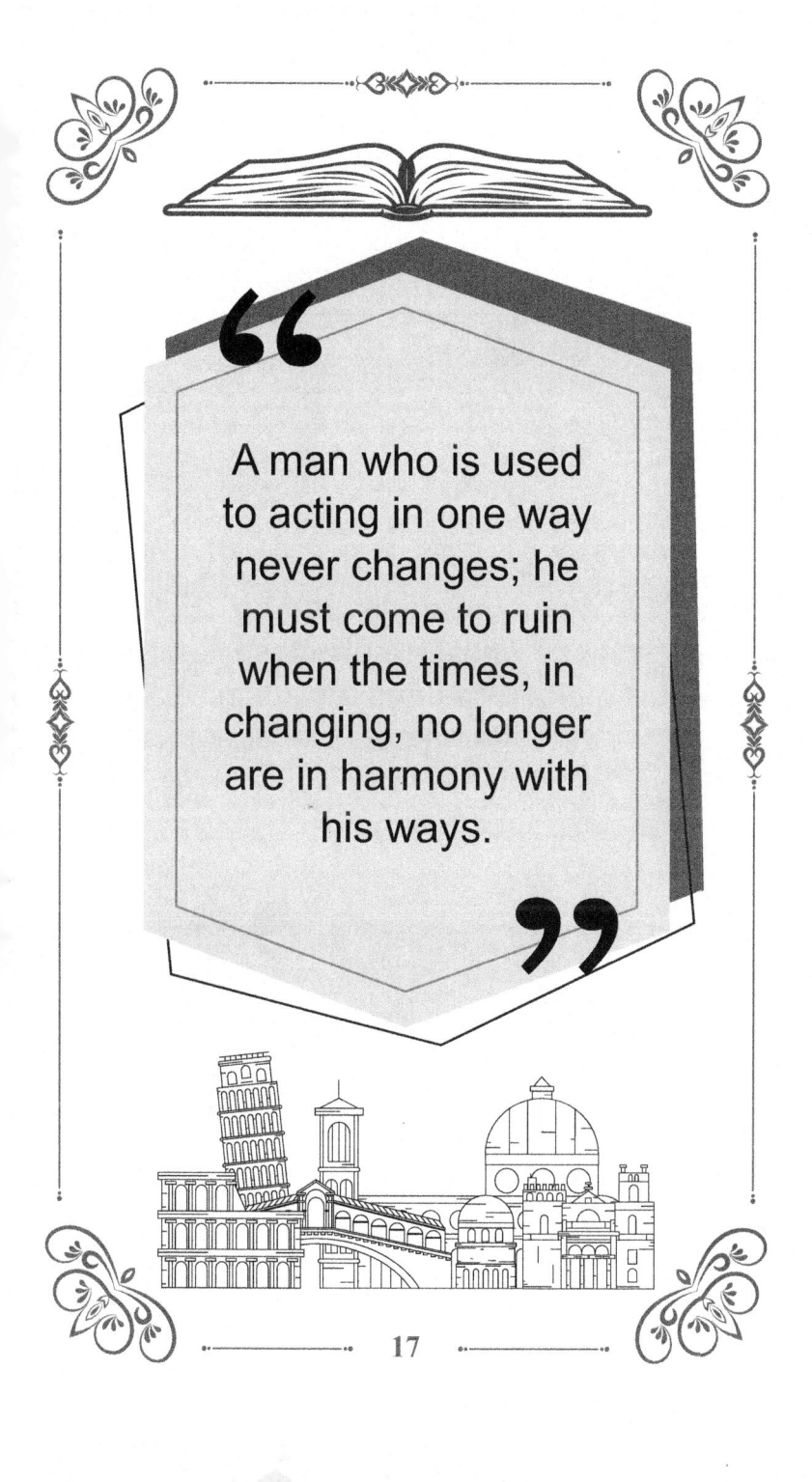

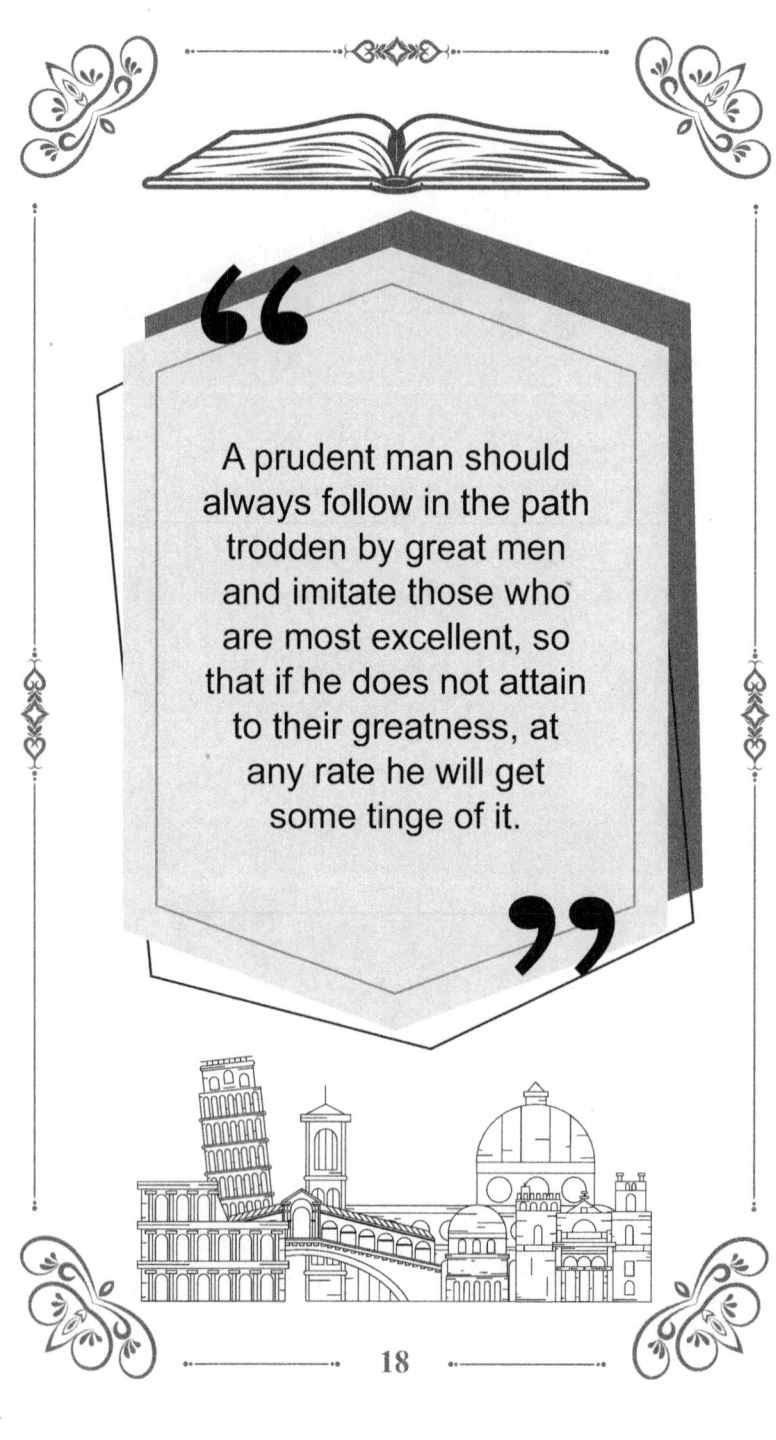

> A prudent man should always follow in the path trodden by great men and imitate those who are most excellent, so that if he does not attain to their greatness, at any rate he will get some tinge of it.

> There is nothing more important than appearing to be religious.

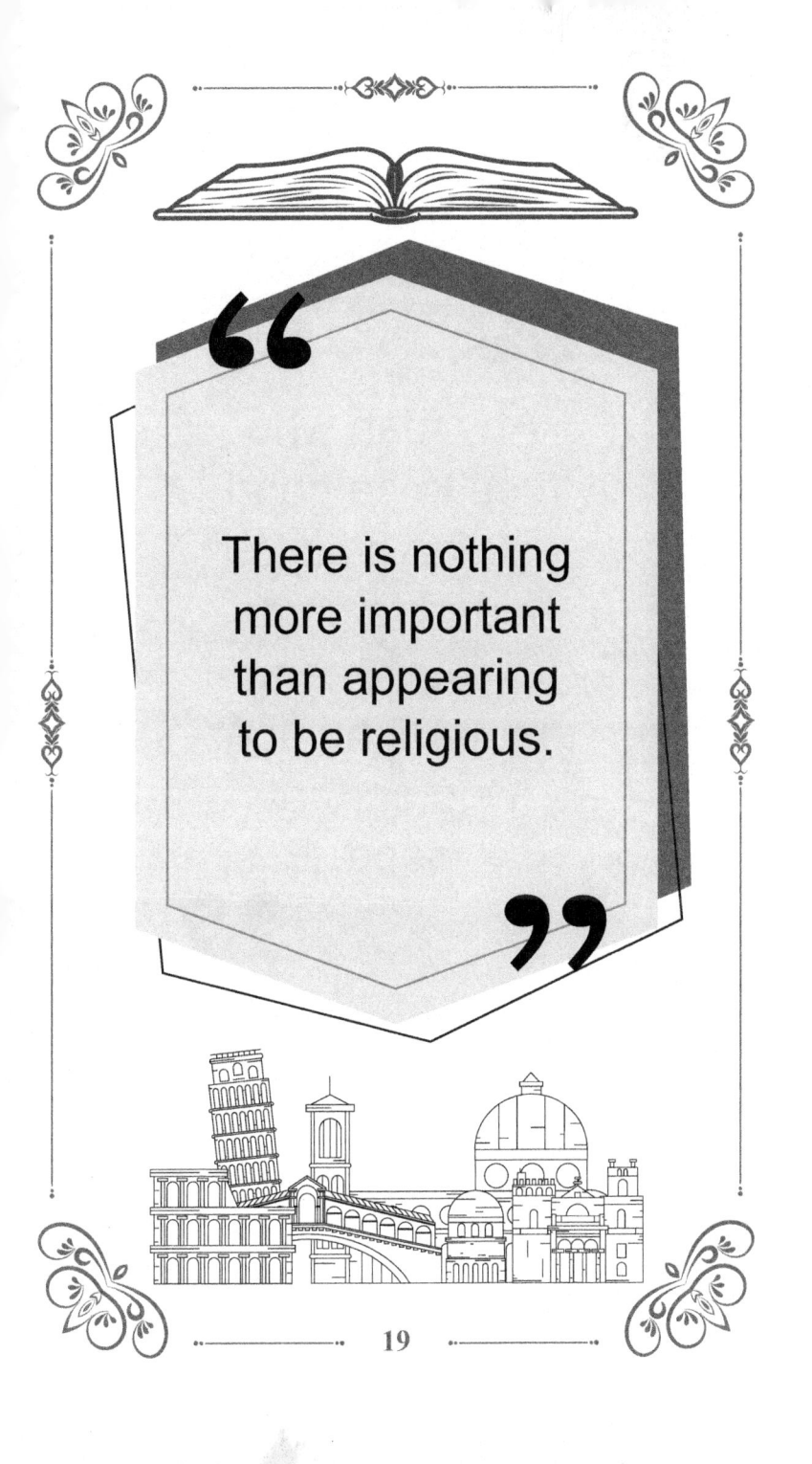

> Any man who tries to be good all the time is bound to come to ruin among the great number who are not good.

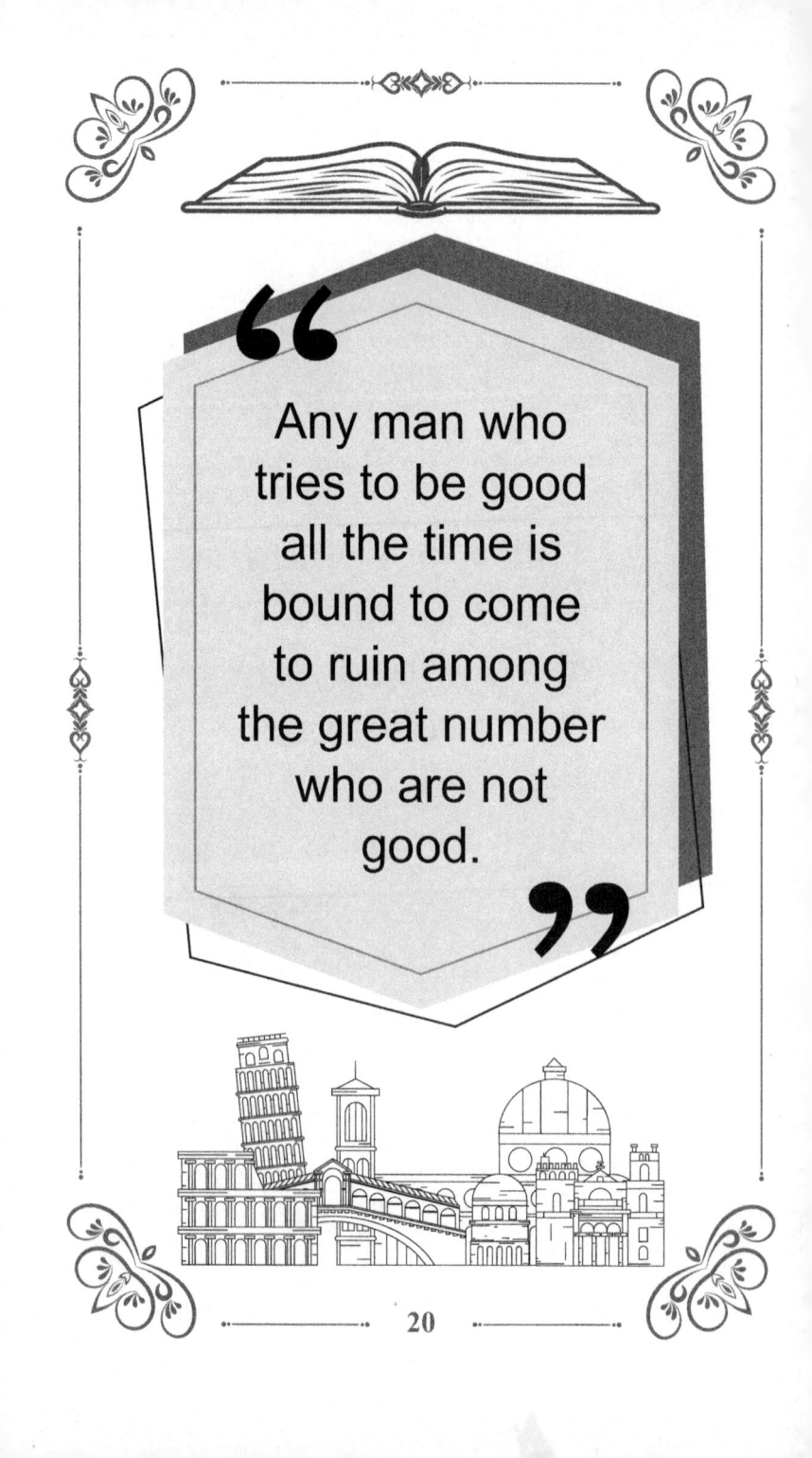

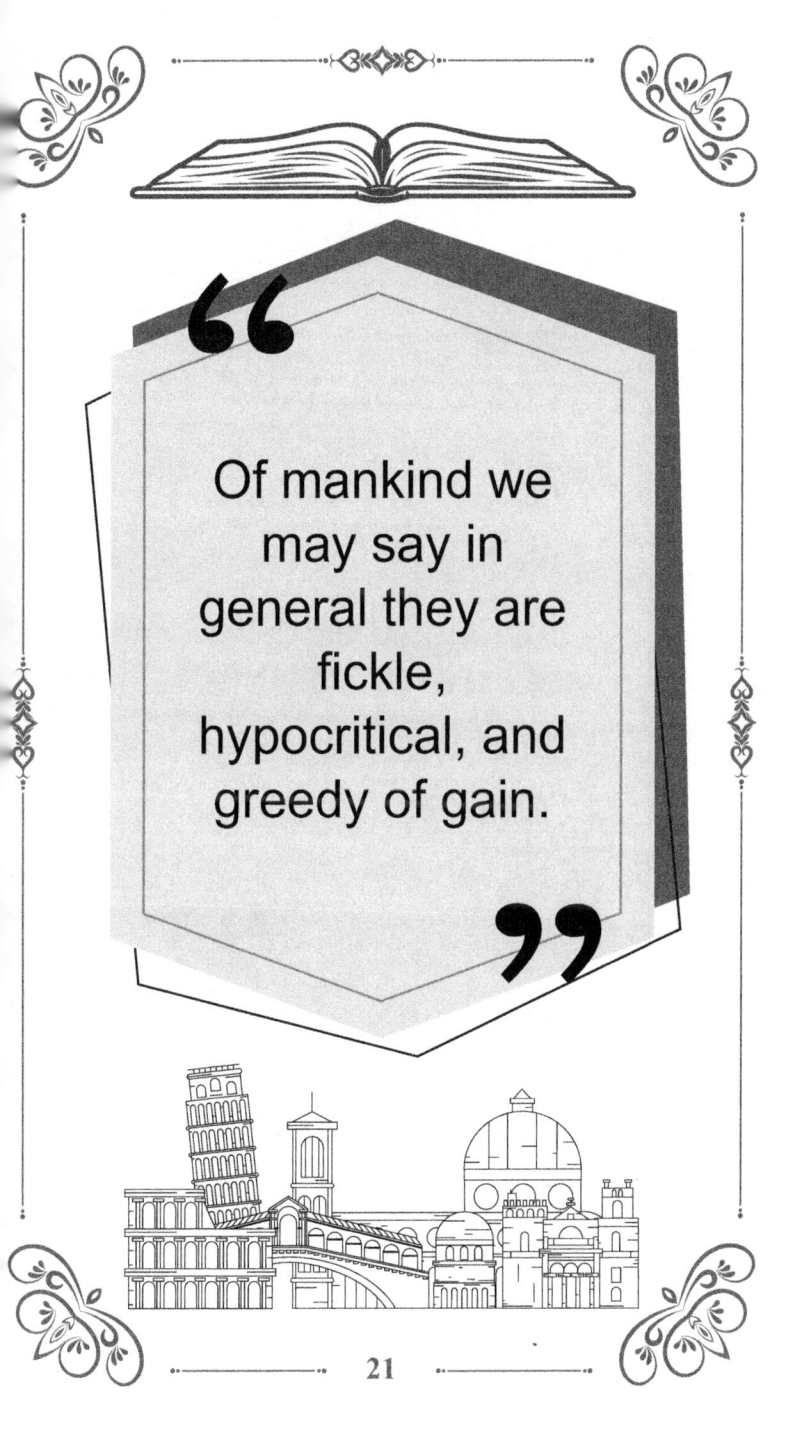

> Of mankind we may say in general they are fickle, hypocritical, and greedy of gain.

> Wisdom consists of knowing how to distinguish the nature of trouble, and in choosing the lesser evil.

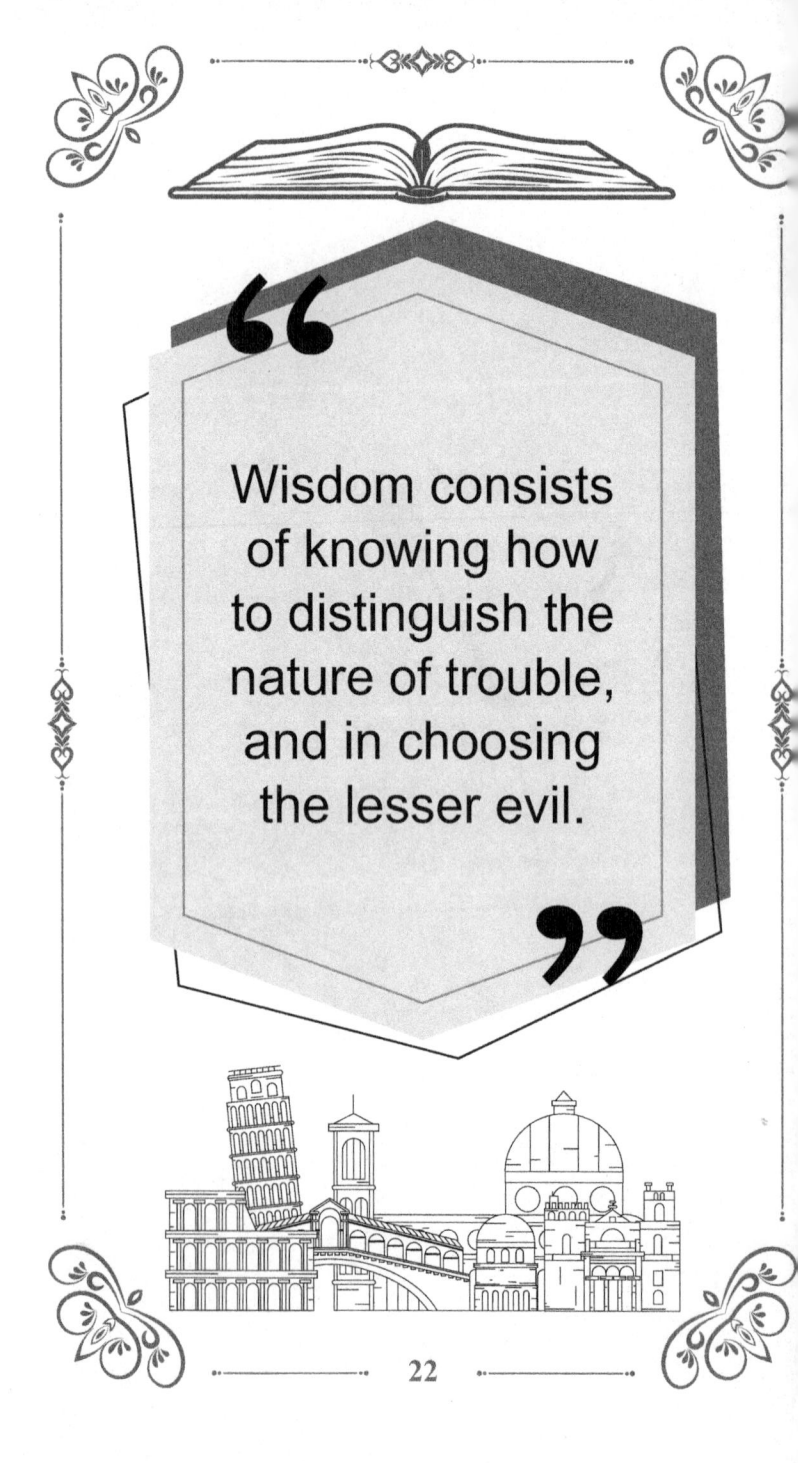

> It must be considered that there is nothing more difficult to carry out, nor more doubtful of success, nor more dangerous to handle, than to initiate a new order of things.

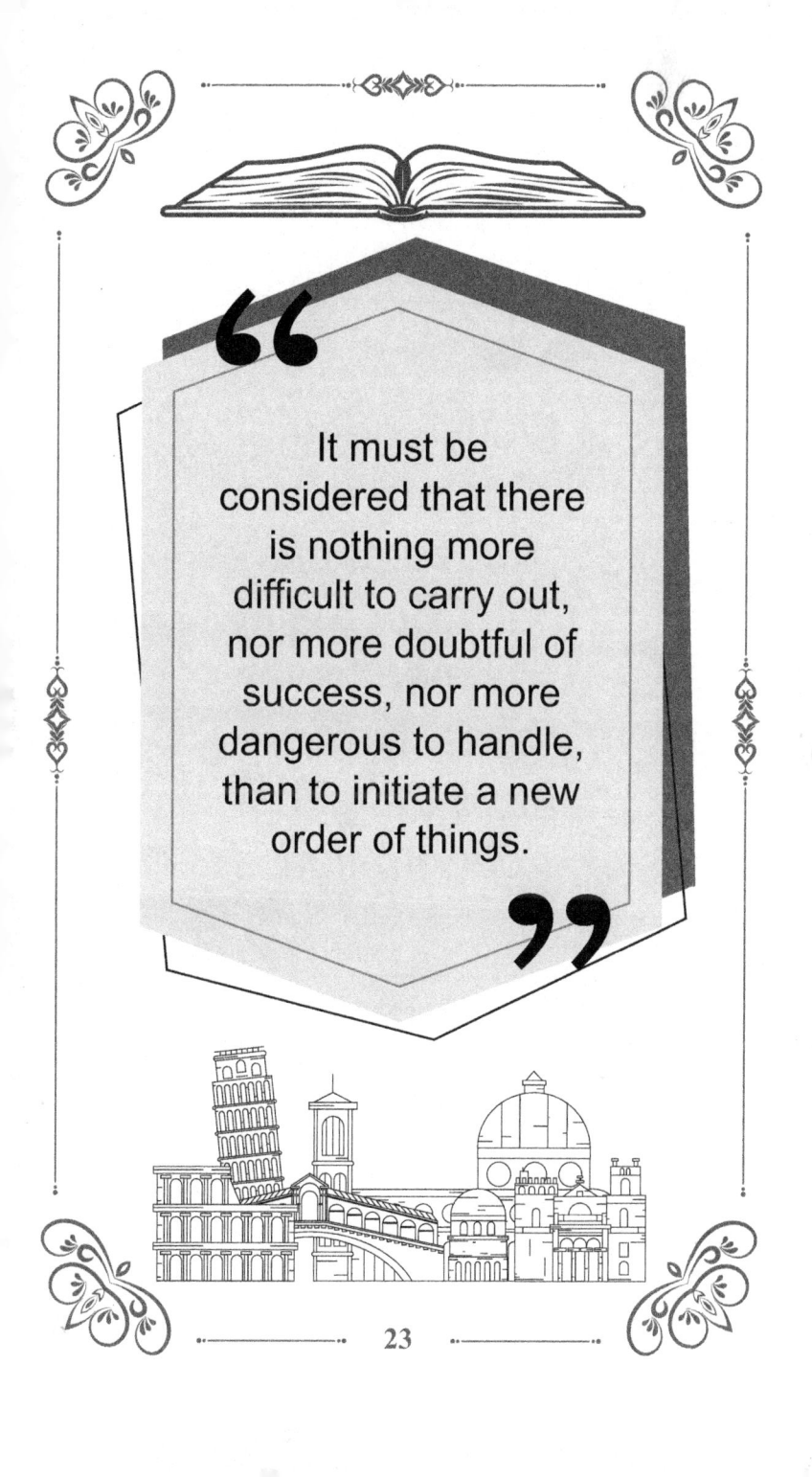

> Men in general judge more from appearances than from reality. All men have eyes, but few have the gift of penetration.

> He who becomes a prince through the favor of the people should always keep on good terms with them; which it is easy for him to do, since all they ask is not to be oppressed.

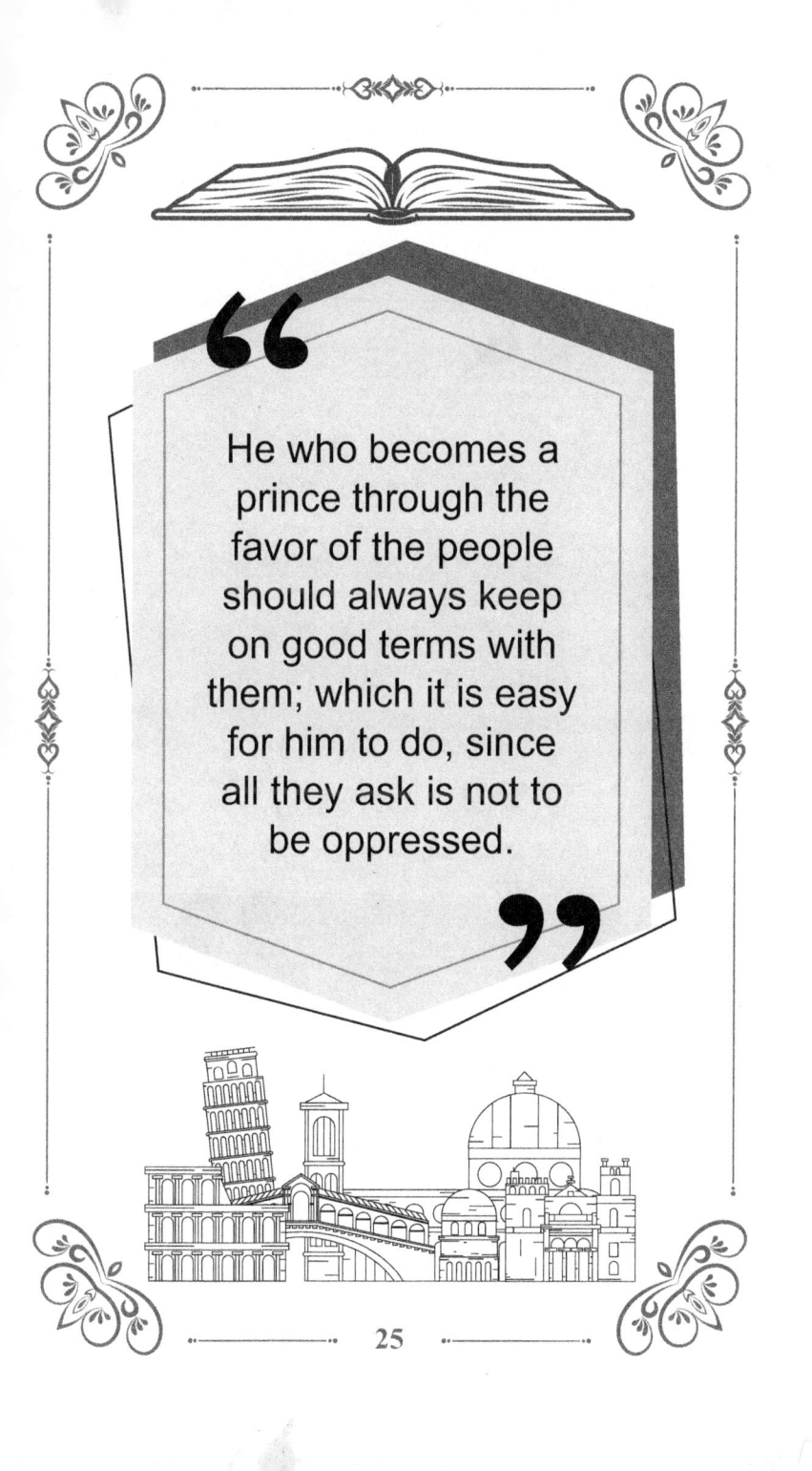

> There is no avoiding war, it can only be postponed to the advantage of your enemy.

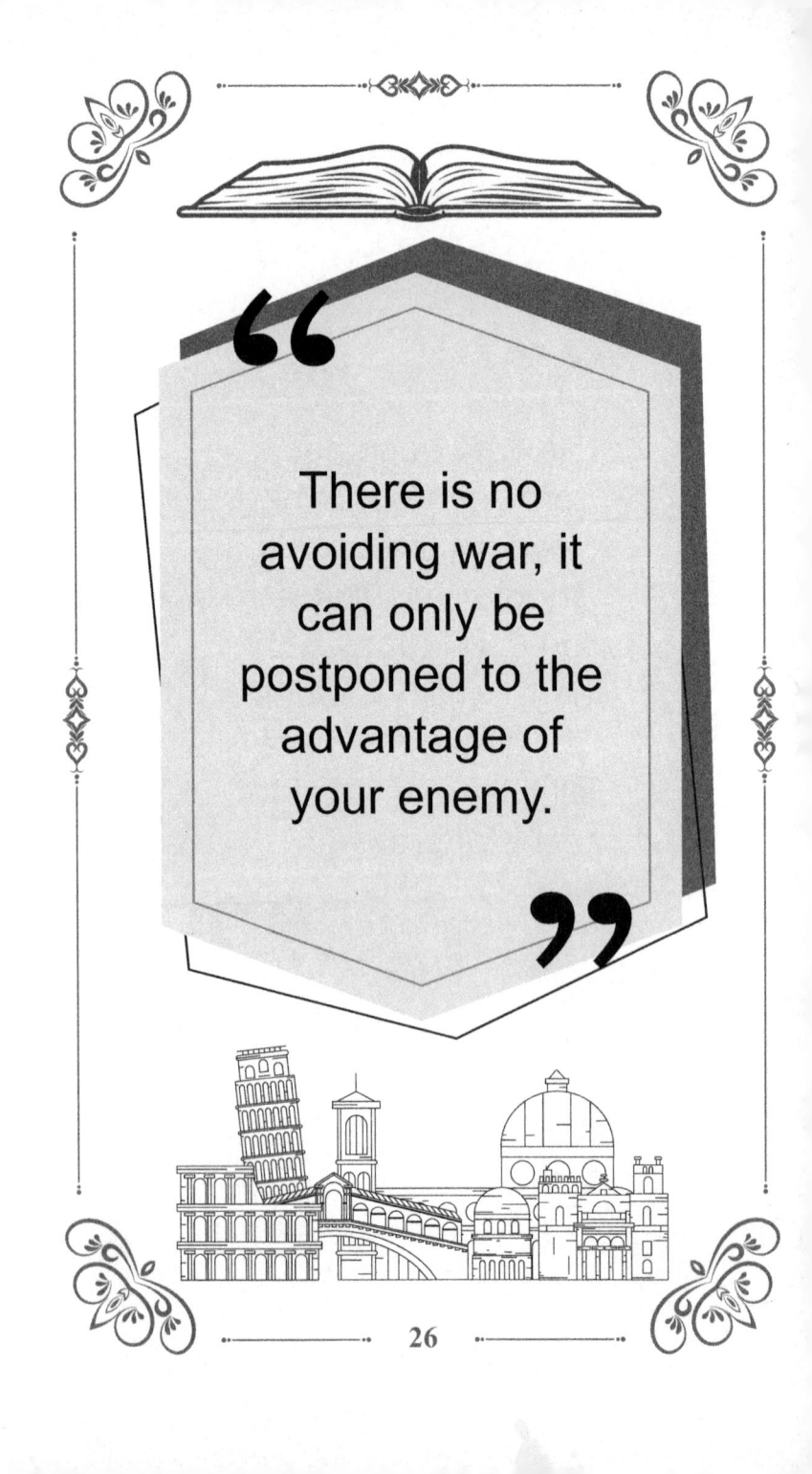

> It is better to act and repent than not to act and regret.

> The arms of others either fall from your back, or they weigh you down, or they bind you fast.

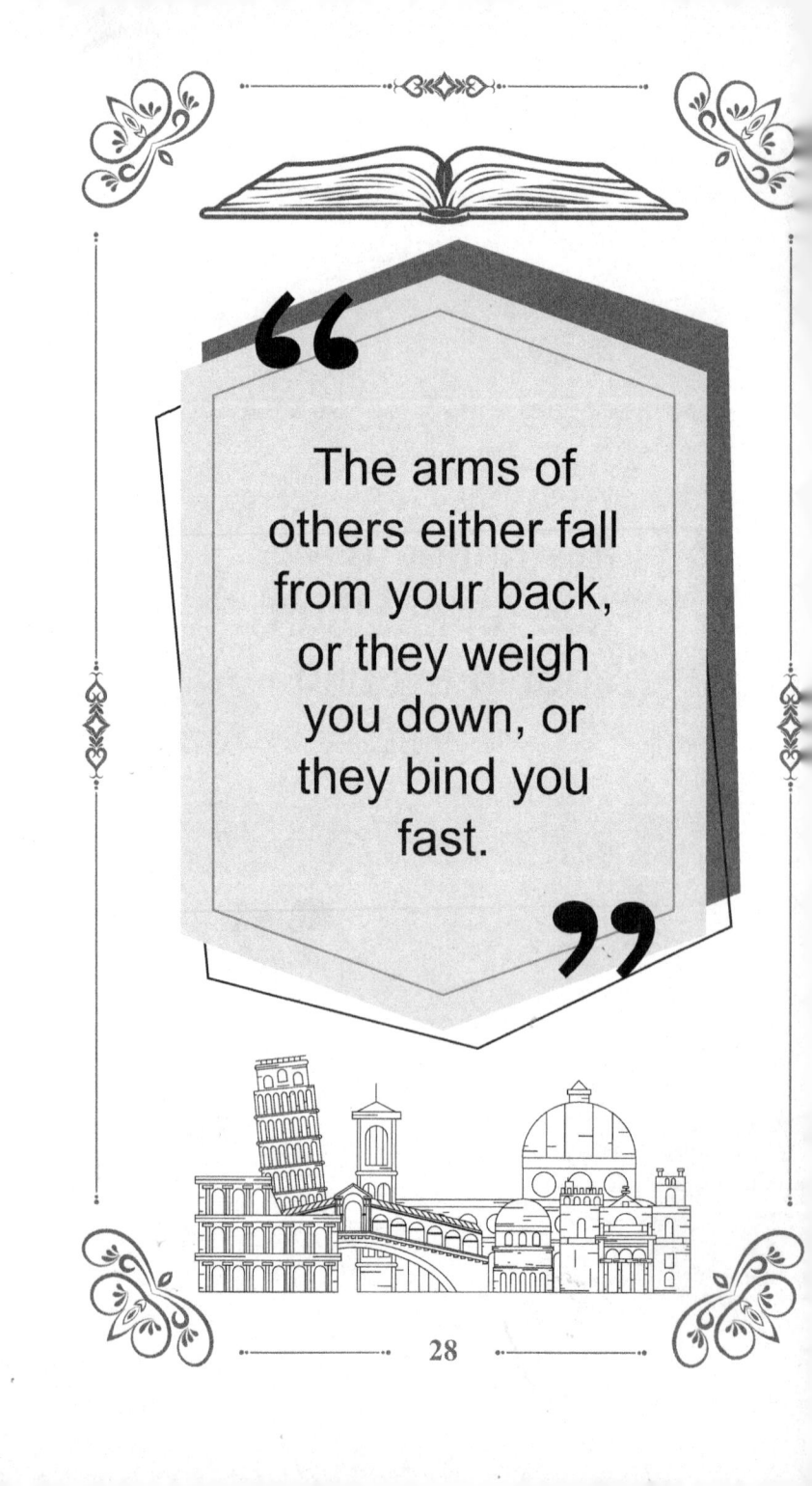

> He who builds on the people, builds on the mud.

> Nature creates few men brave, industry and training makes many.

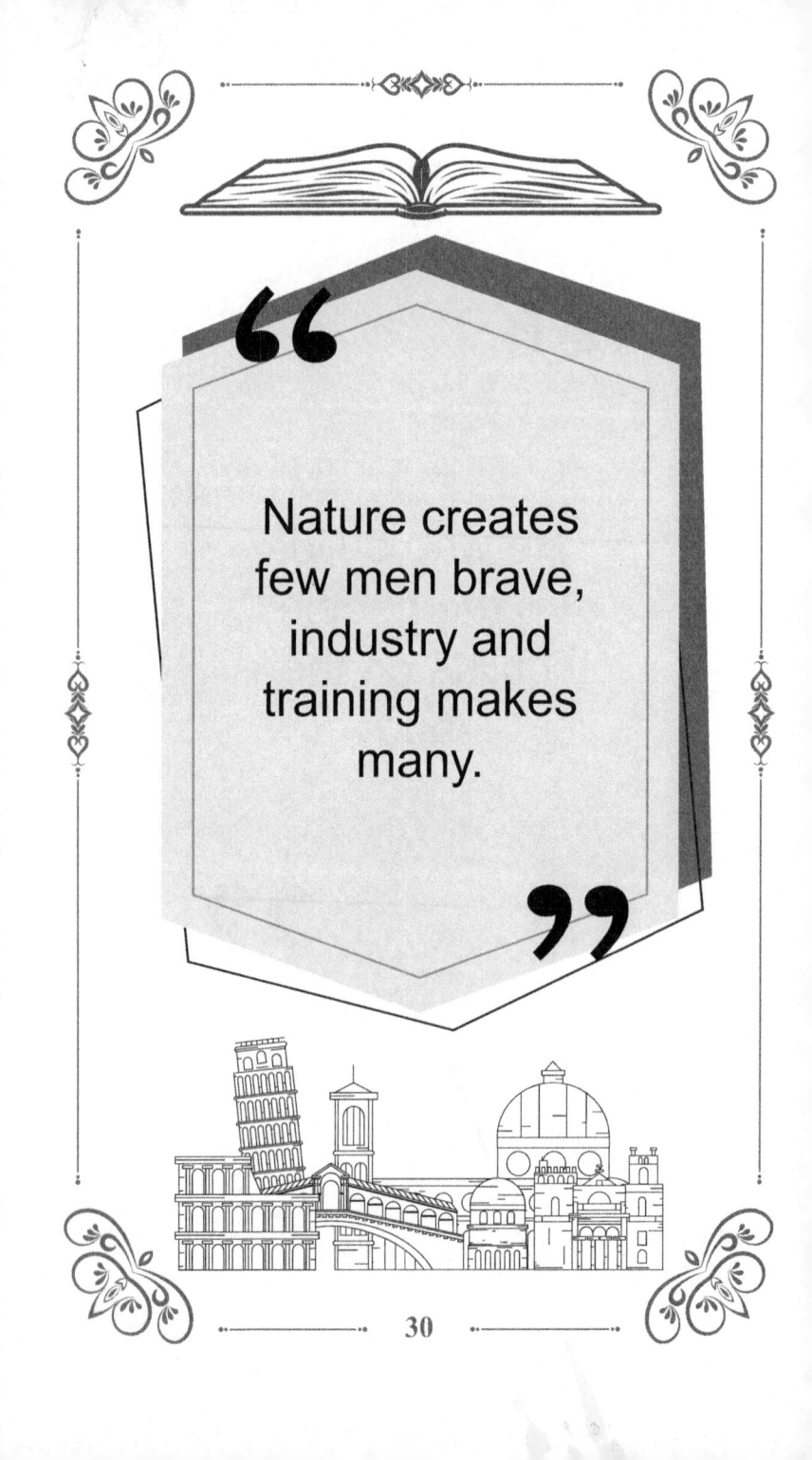

> Everyone who wants to know what will happen ought to examine what has happened: everything in this world in any epoch has their replicas in antiquity.

> Men never do good unless necessity drives them to it; but when they are free to choose and can do just as they please, confusion and disorder become rampant.

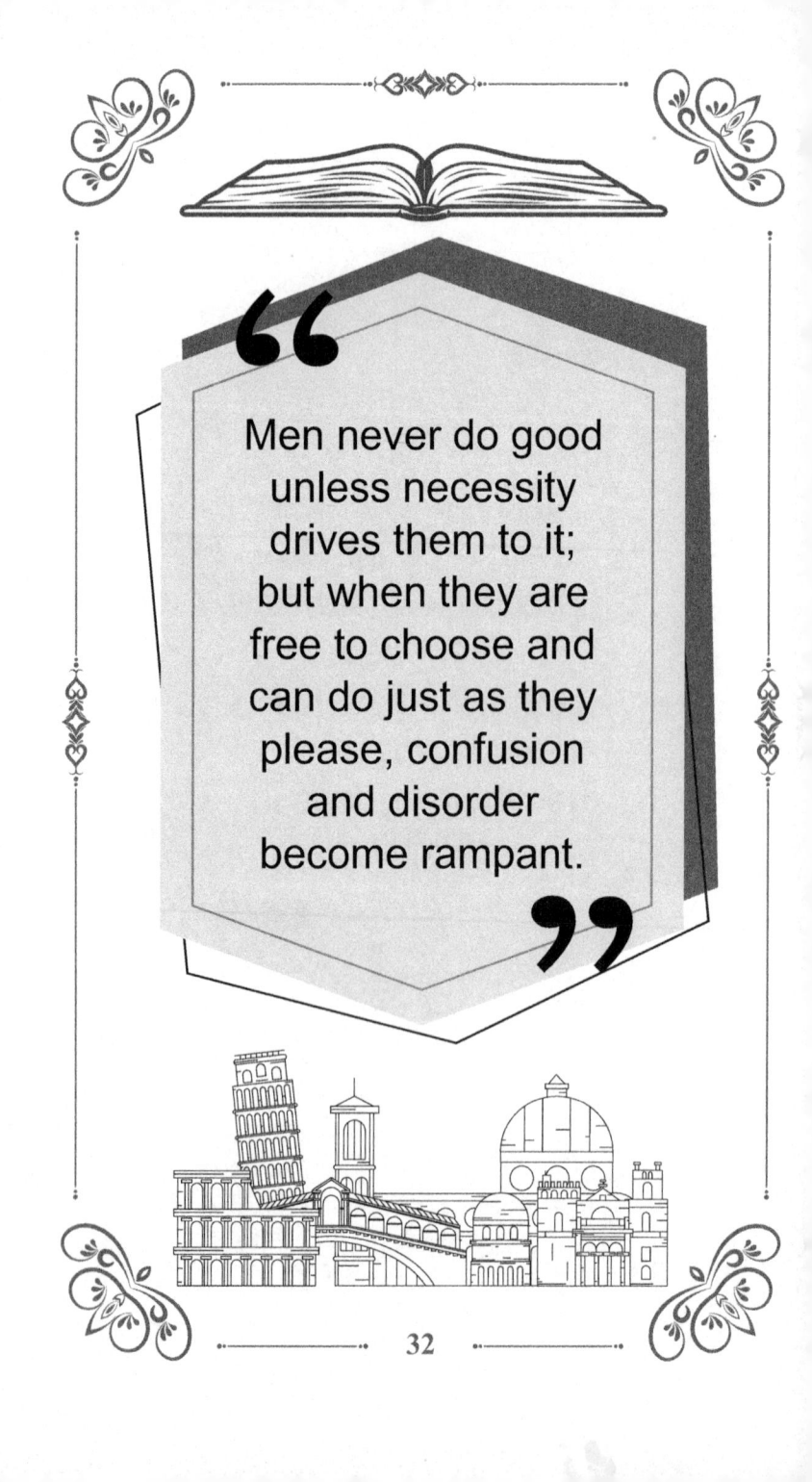

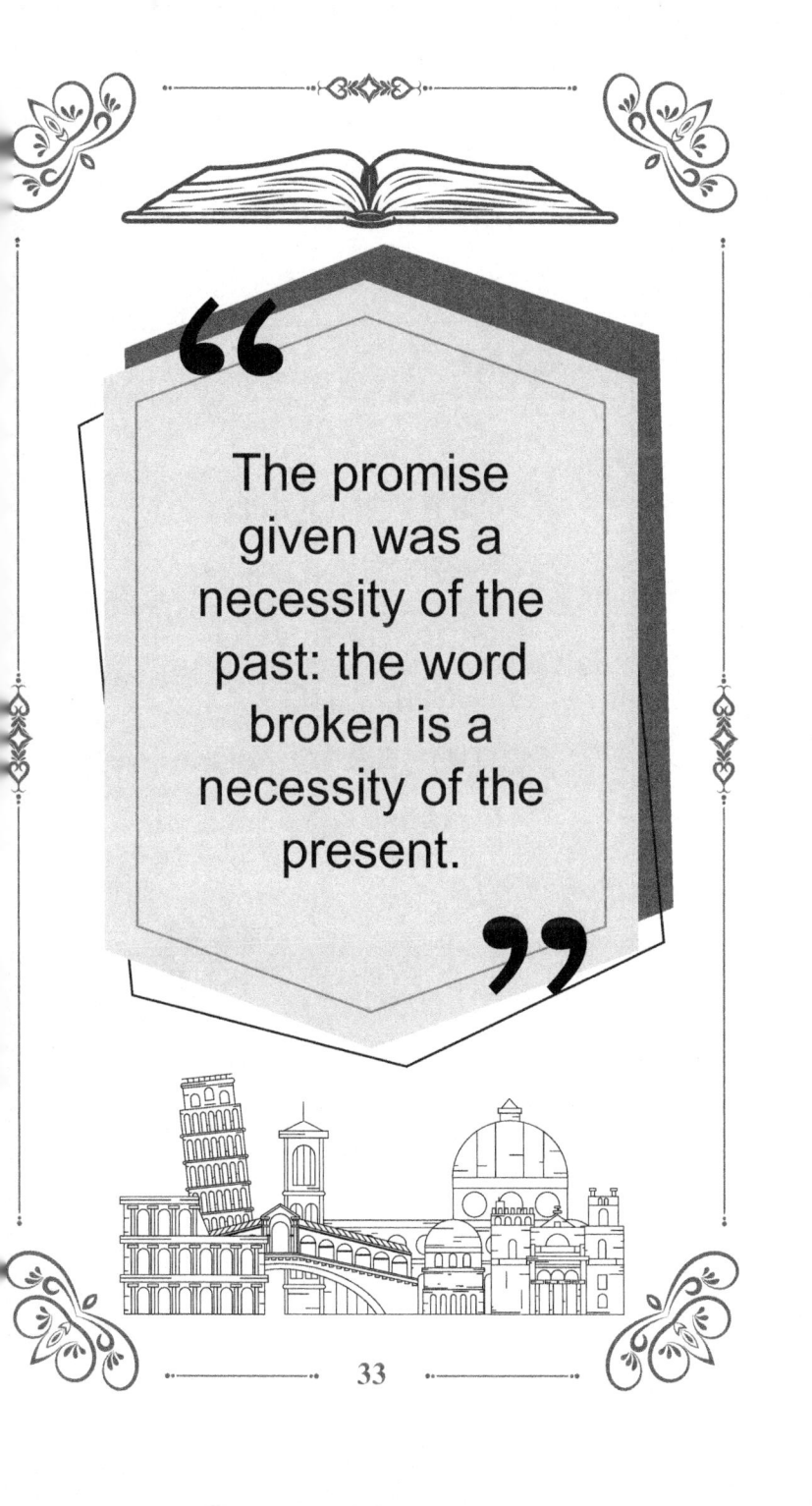

"The promise given was a necessity of the past: the word broken is a necessity of the present."

> One should never fall in the belief that you can find someone to pick you up.

> He who is highly esteemed is not easily conspired against.

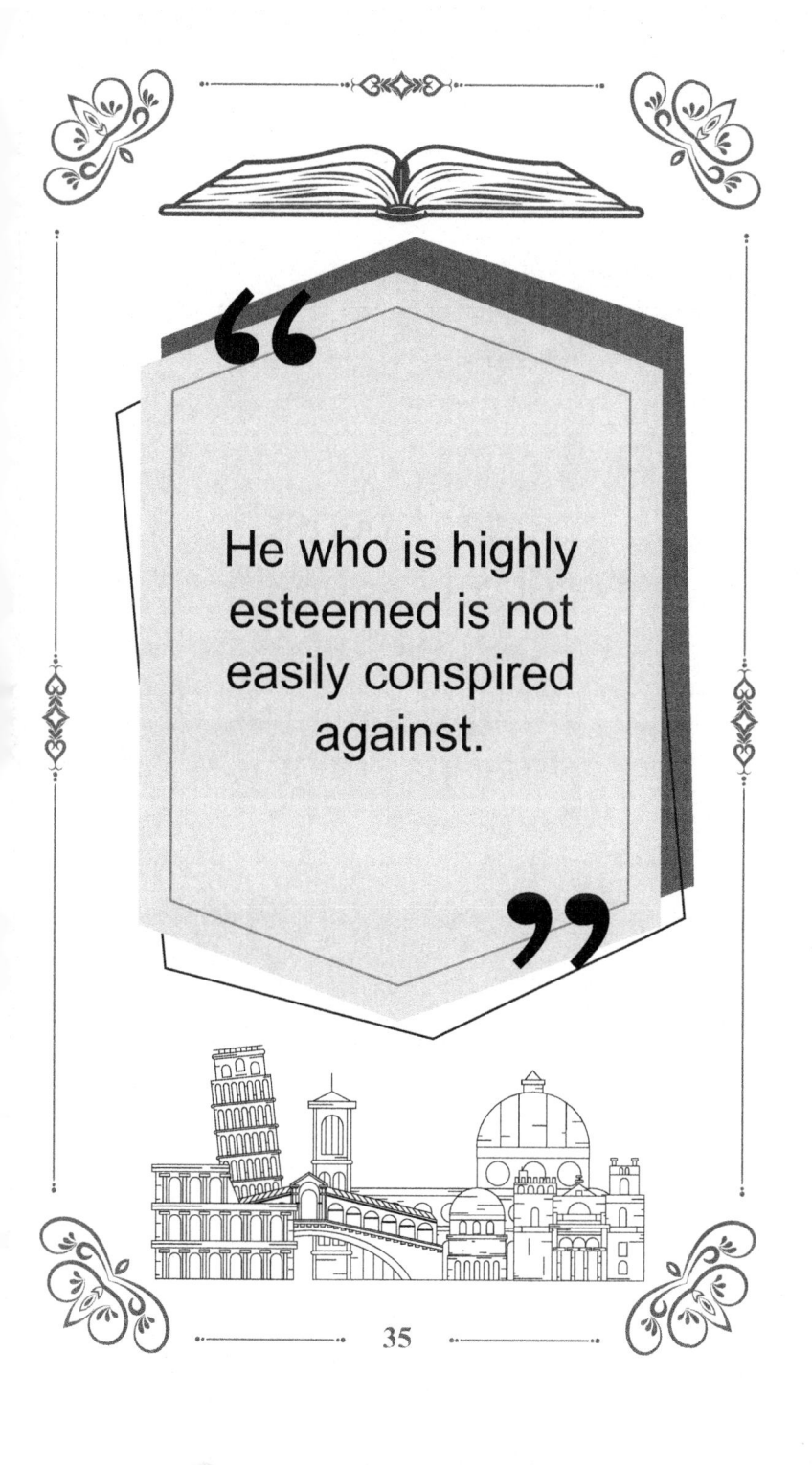

> Men sooner forget the death of their father than the loss of their patrimony.

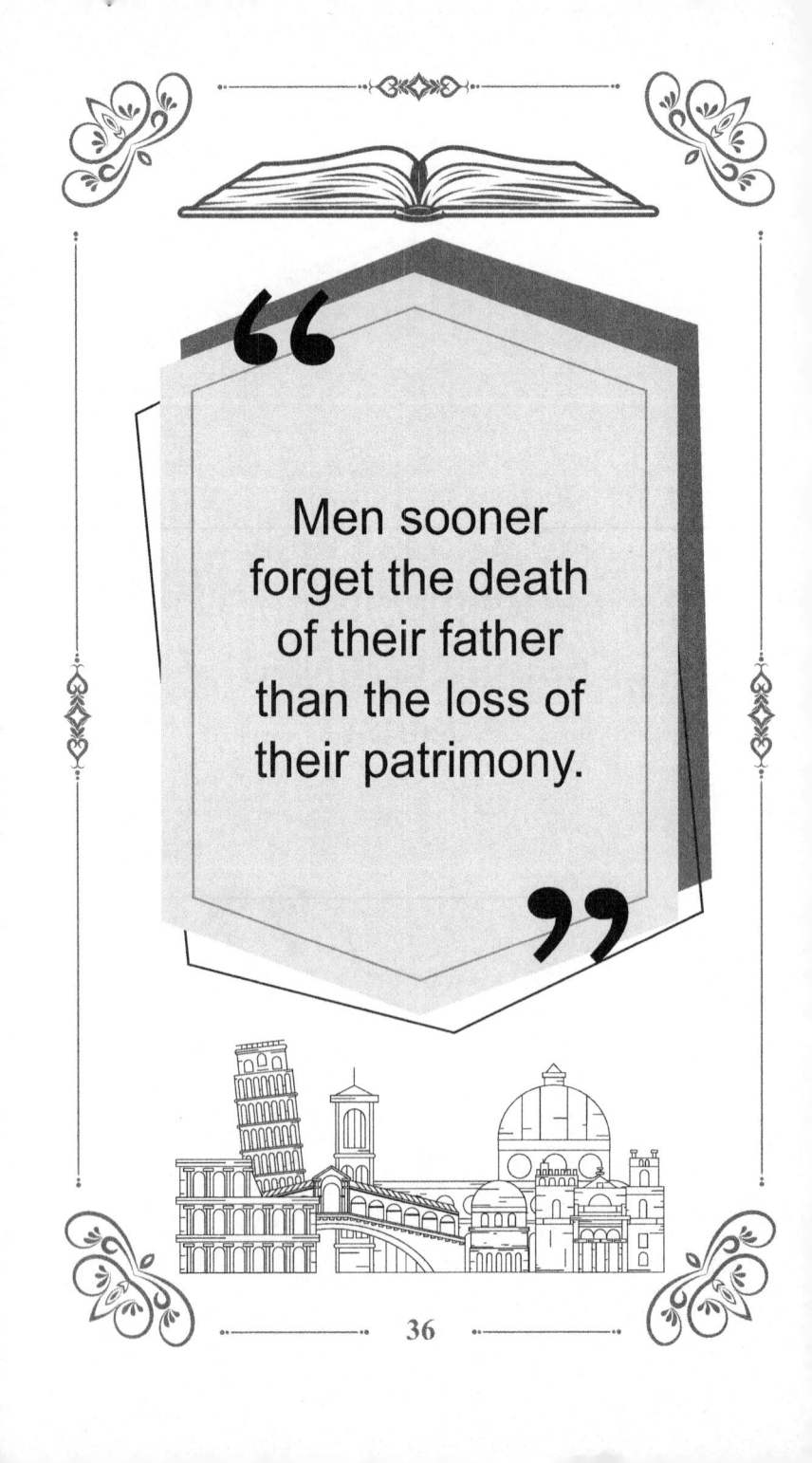

> Therefore the best fortress is to be found in the love of the people, for although you may have fortresses they will not save you if you are hated by the people.

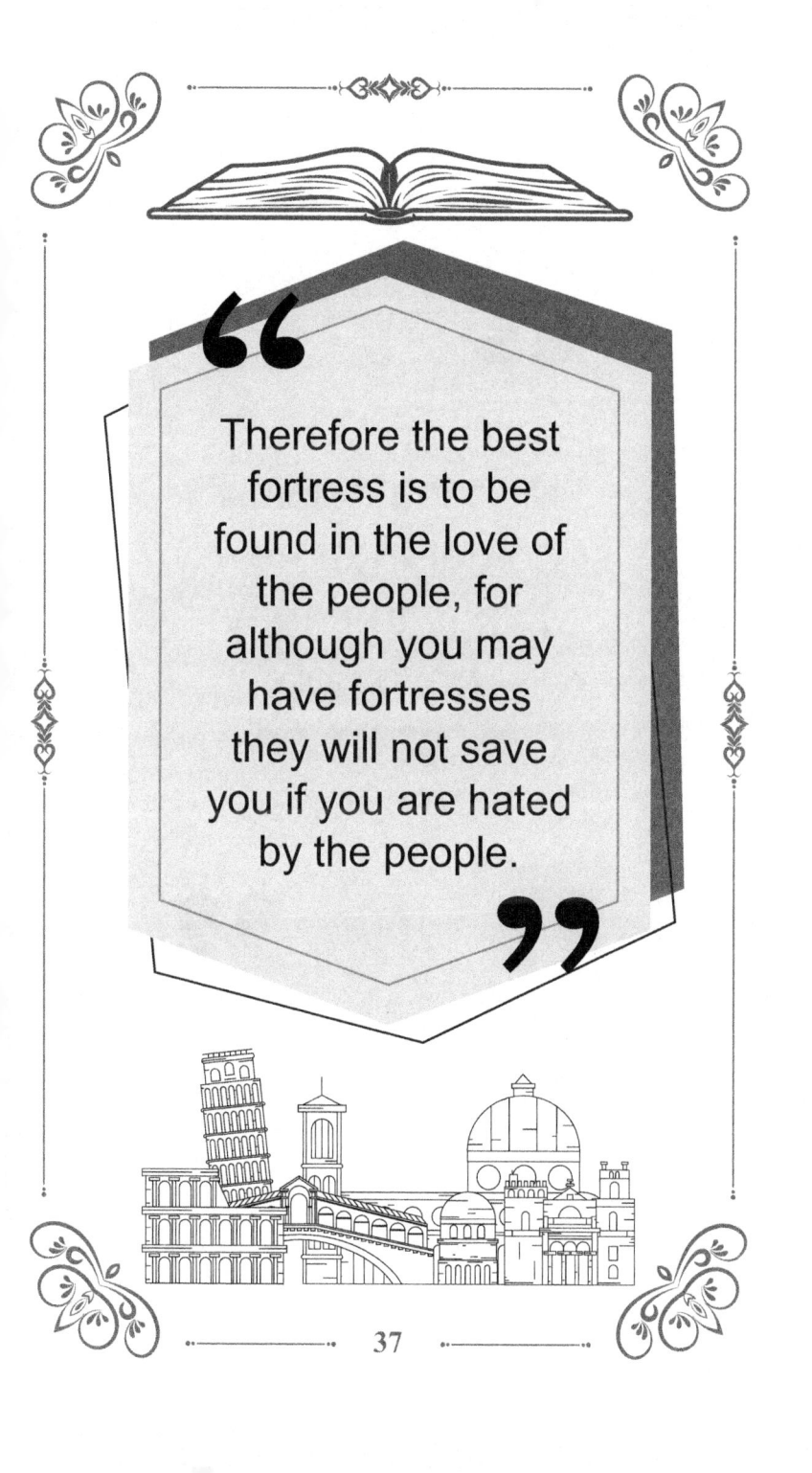

> Men intrinsically do not trust new things that they have not experienced themselves.

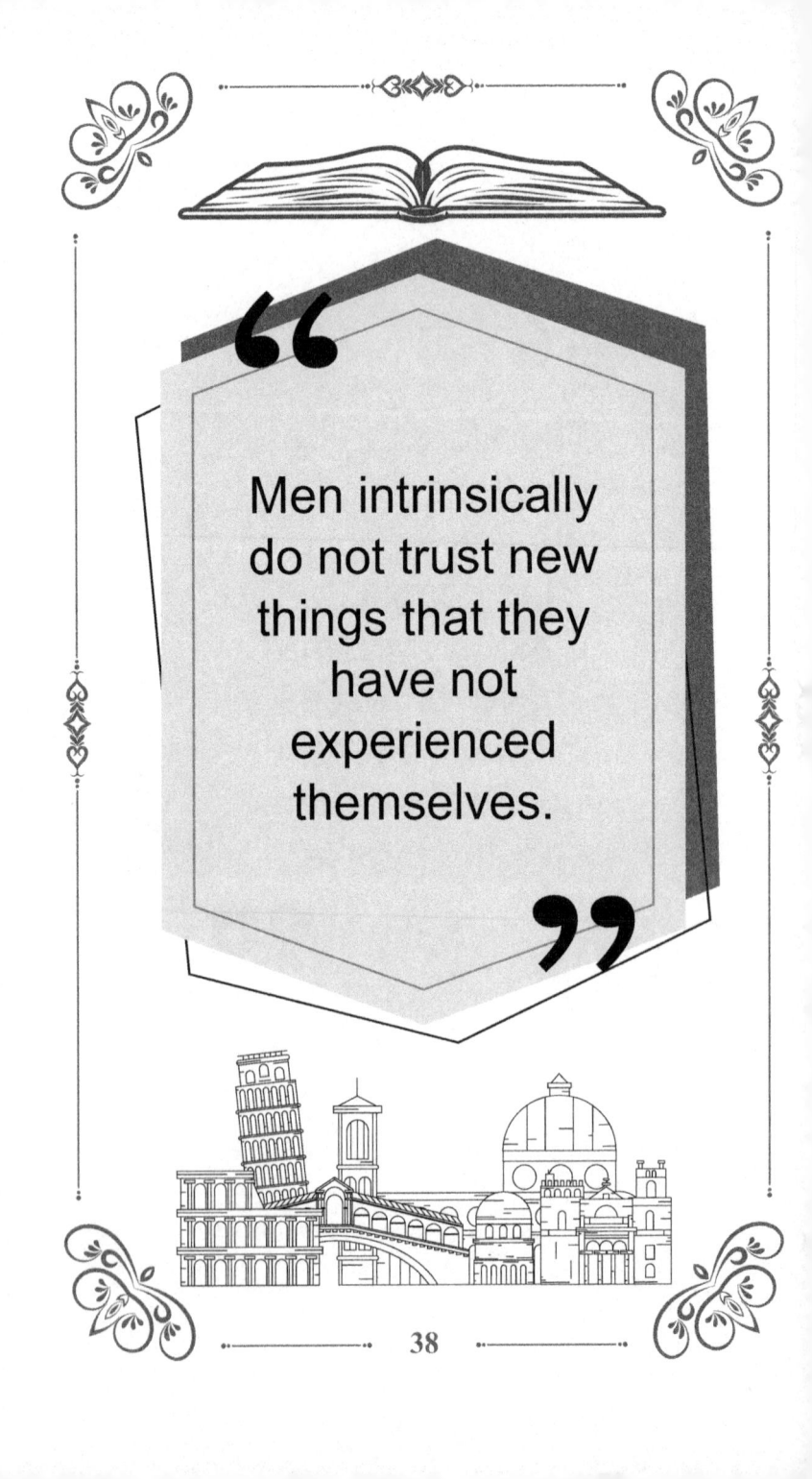

> It is double pleasure to deceive the deceiver.

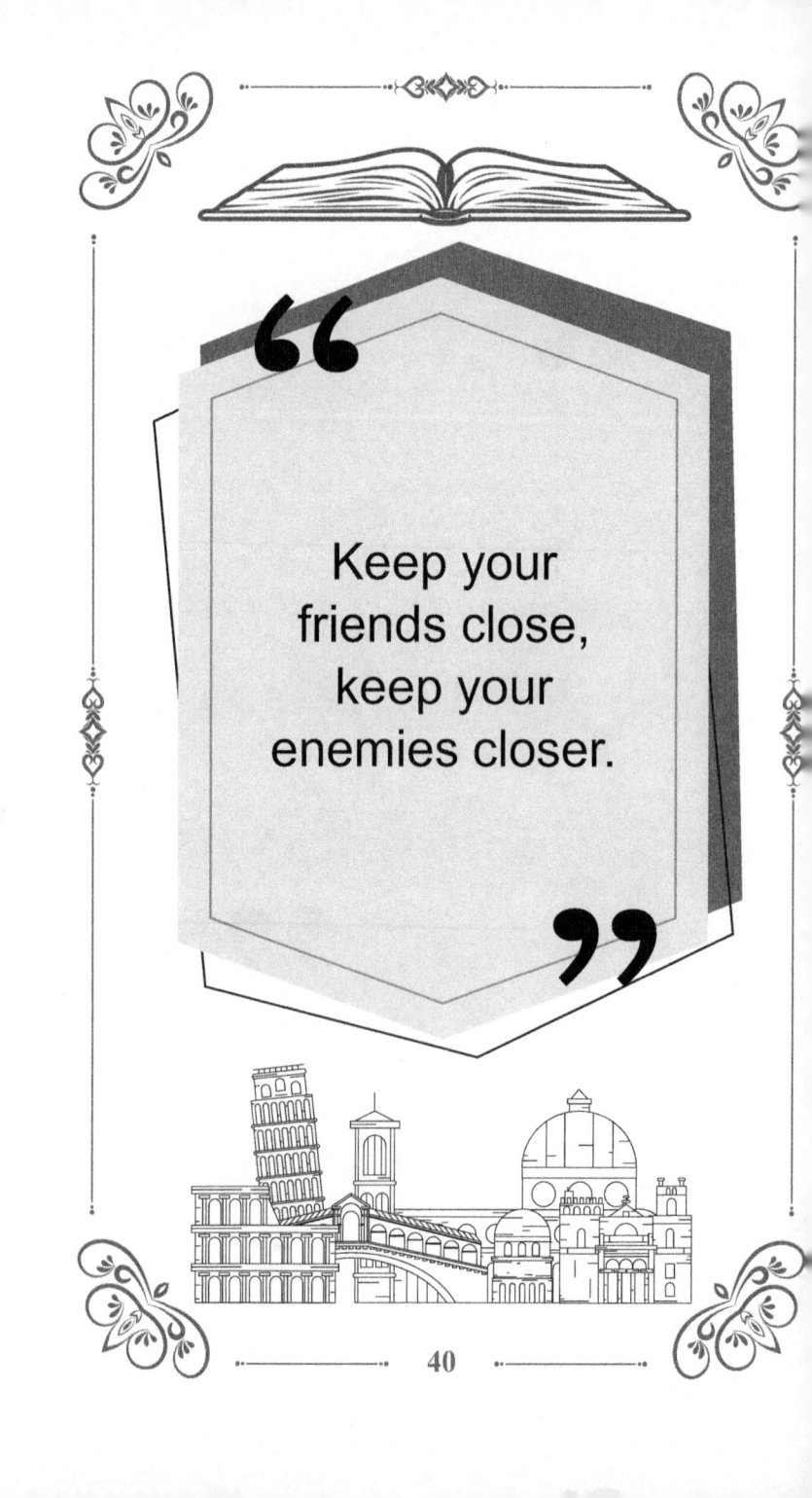

"Keep your friends close, keep your enemies closer."

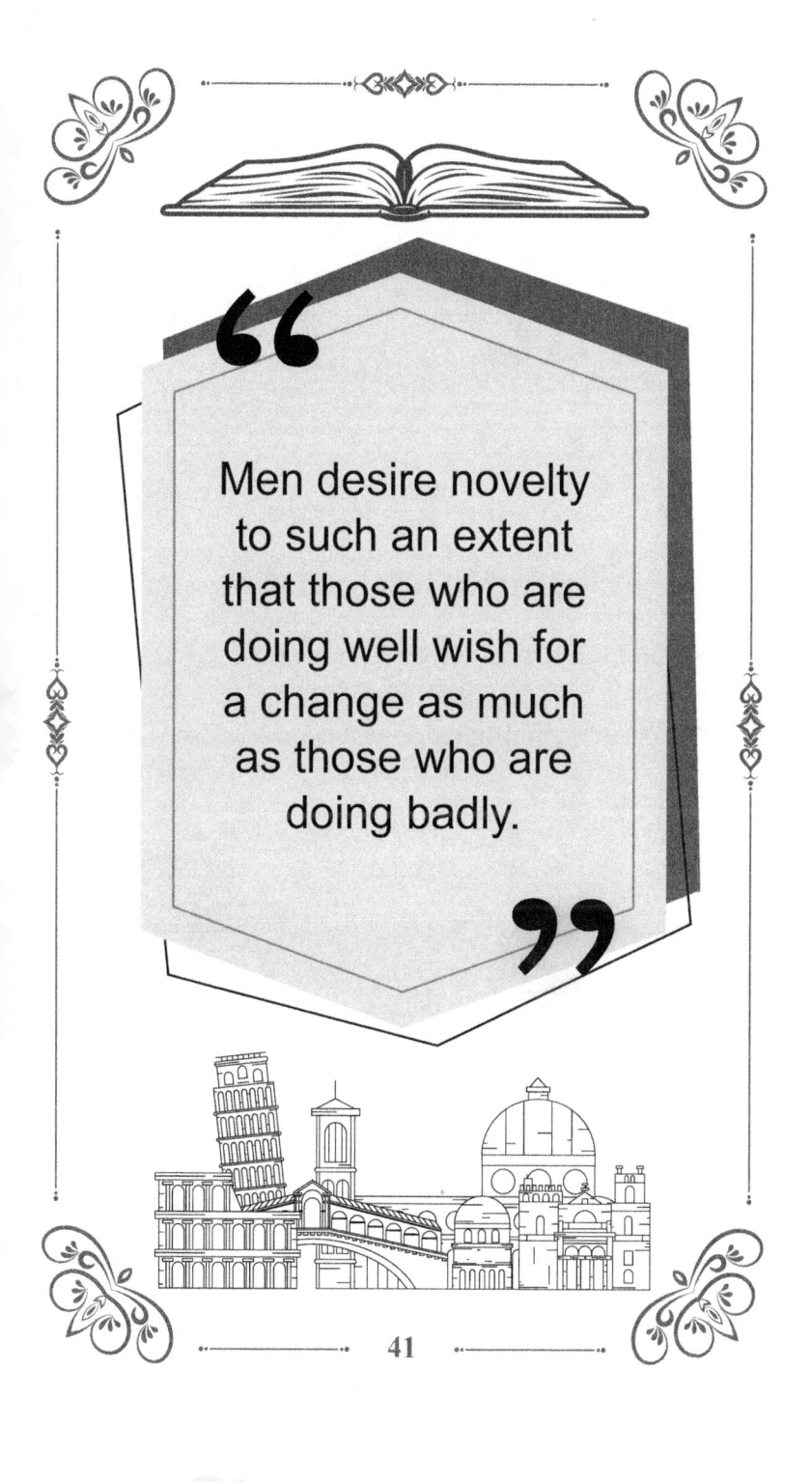

> Men desire novelty to such an extent that those who are doing well wish for a change as much as those who are doing badly.

> A prince is also esteemed when he is a true friend and a true enemy.

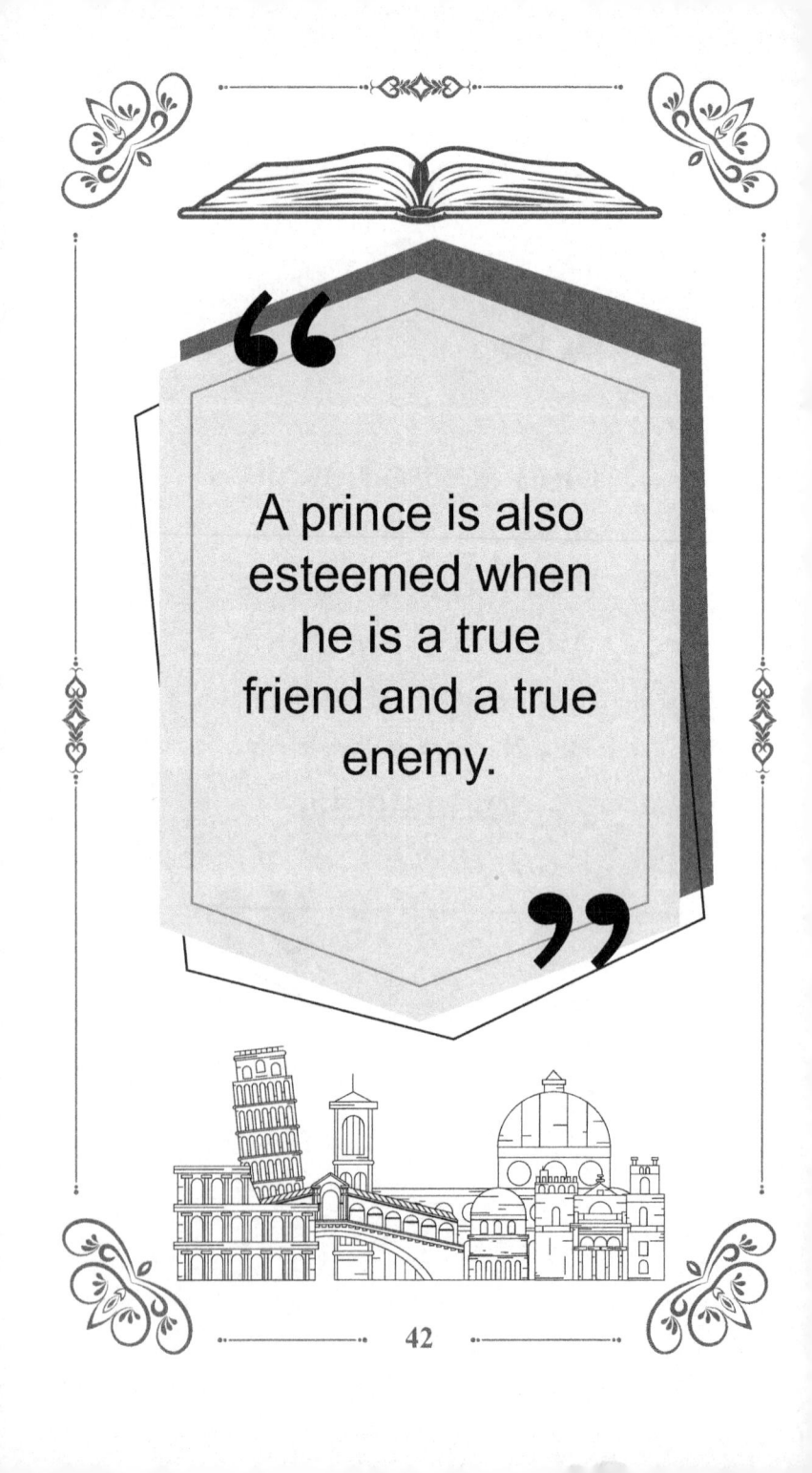

> I desire to go to Hell and not to Heaven. In the former I shall enjoy the company of popes, kings and princes, while in the latter are only beggars, monks and apostles.

> For, in truth, there is no sure way of holding other than by destroying.

> It is necessary for a prince wishing to hold his own to know how to do wrong, and to make use of it or not according to necessity.

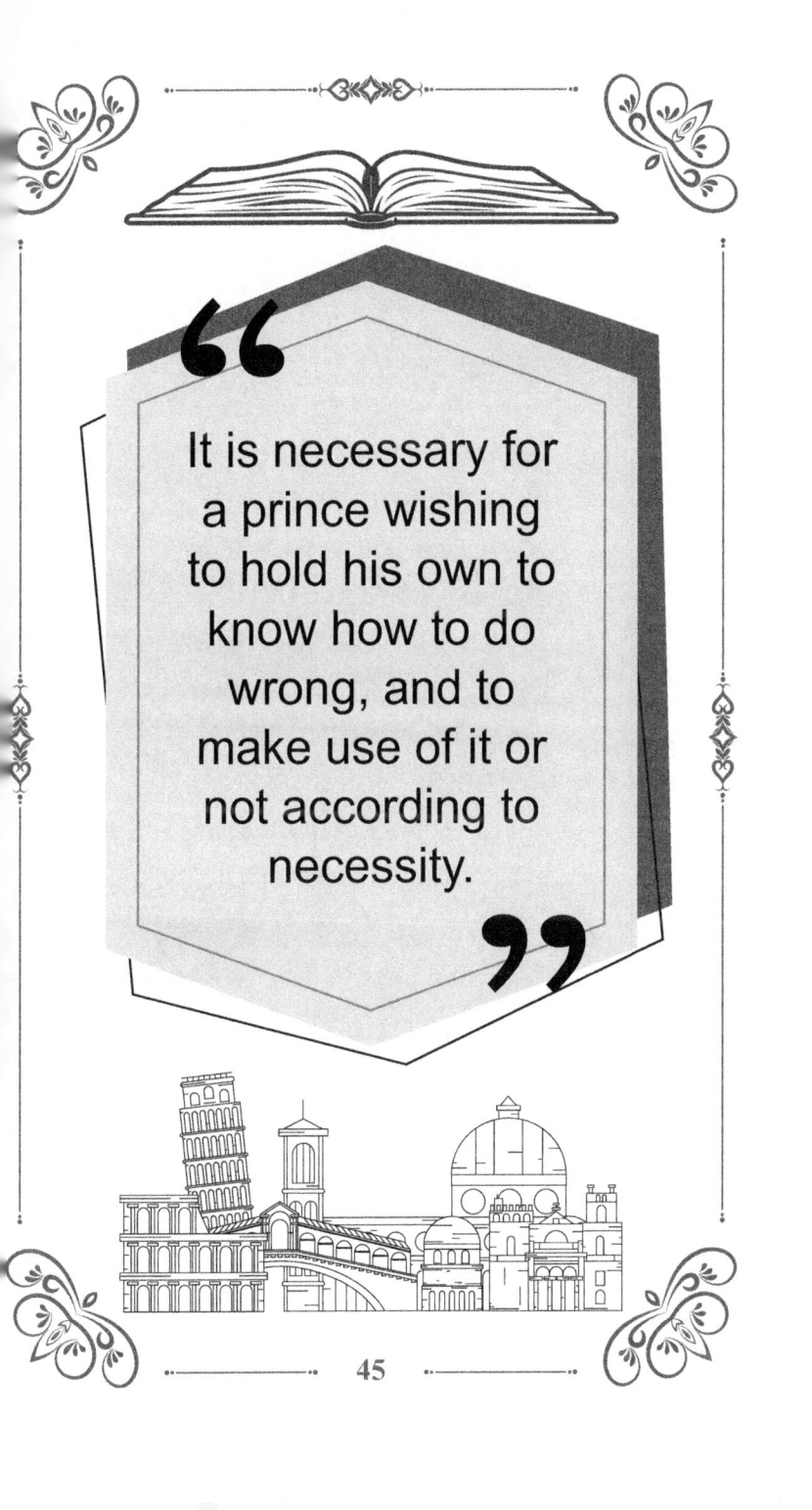

> He who causes another to become powerful ruins himself, for he brings such a power into being either by design or by force, and both of these elements are suspects to the one whom he has made powerful.

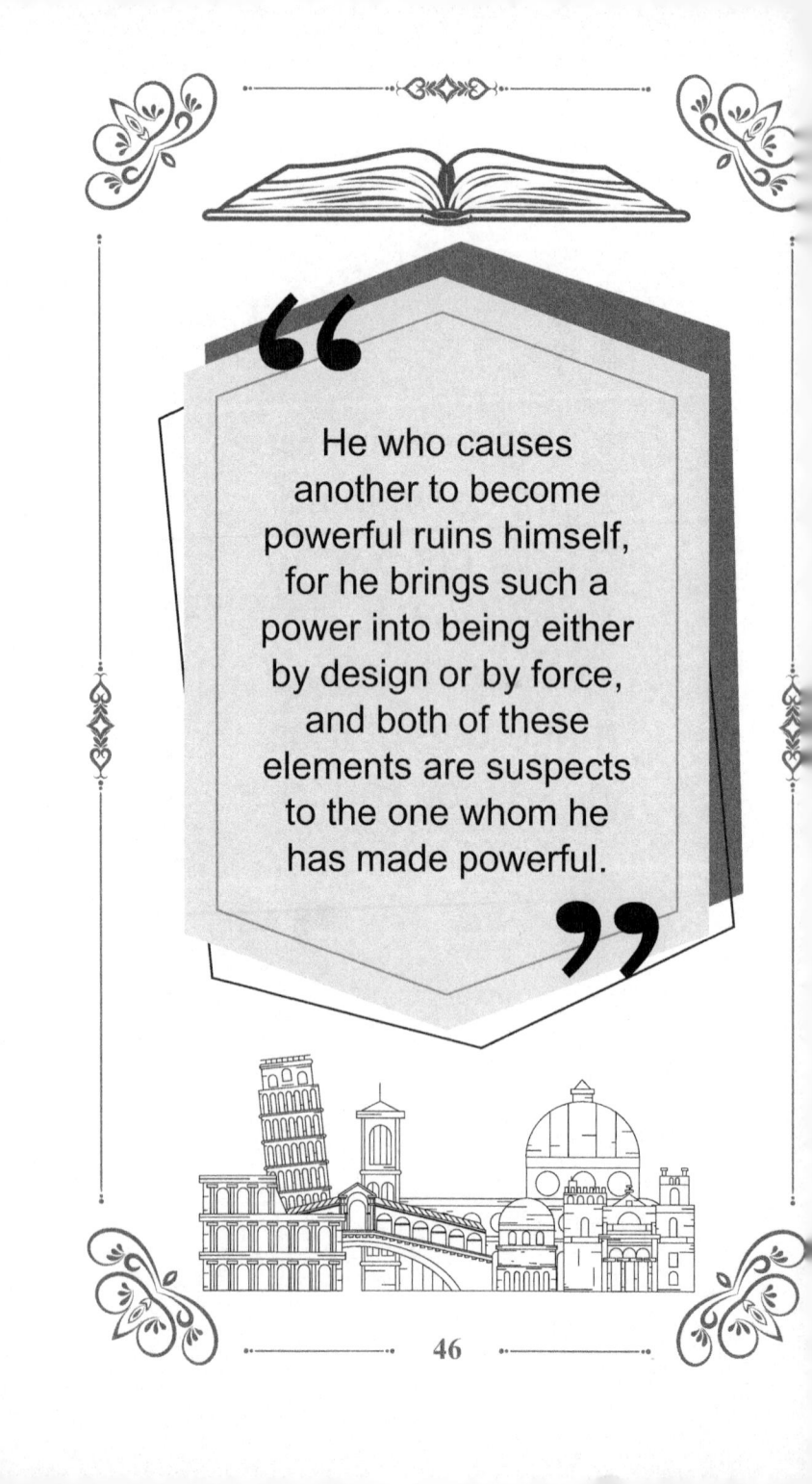

> Being feared and not hated go well together, and the prince can always do this if he does not touch the property or the women of his citizens and subjects.

> For whoever believes that great advancement and new benefits make men forget old injuries is mistaken.

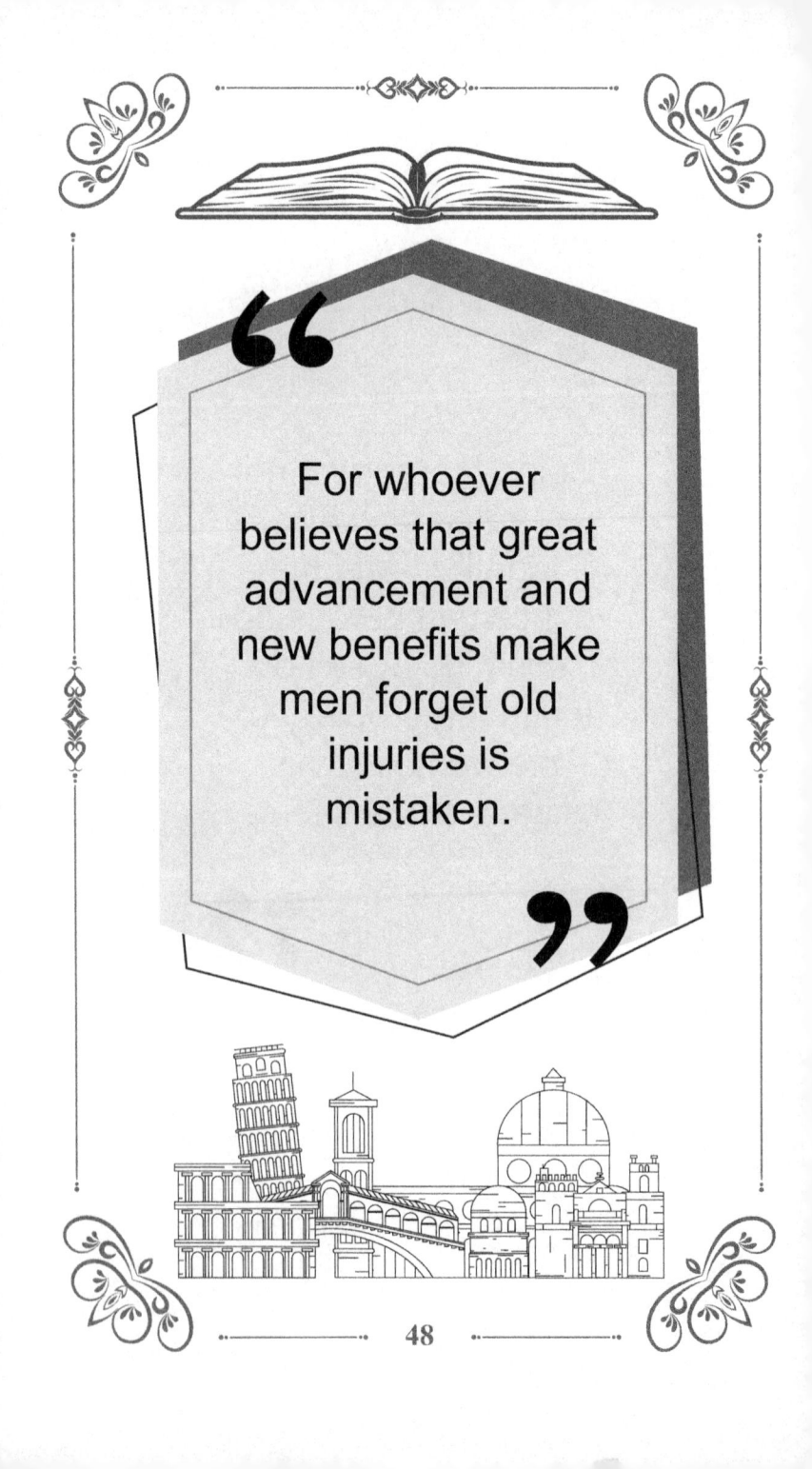

"But when you disarm them, you at once offend them by showing that you distrust them, either for cowardice or for want of loyalty, and either of these opinions breeds hatred against you."

> For, besides what has been said, it should be borne in mind that the temper of the multitude is fickle, and that while it is "easy to persuade them of a thing, it is hard to fix them in that persuasion.

> As the physicians say it happens in hectic fever, that in the beginning of the malady it is easy to cure but difficult to detect, but in the course of time, not having been either detected or treated in the beginning, it becomes easy to detect but difficult to cure.

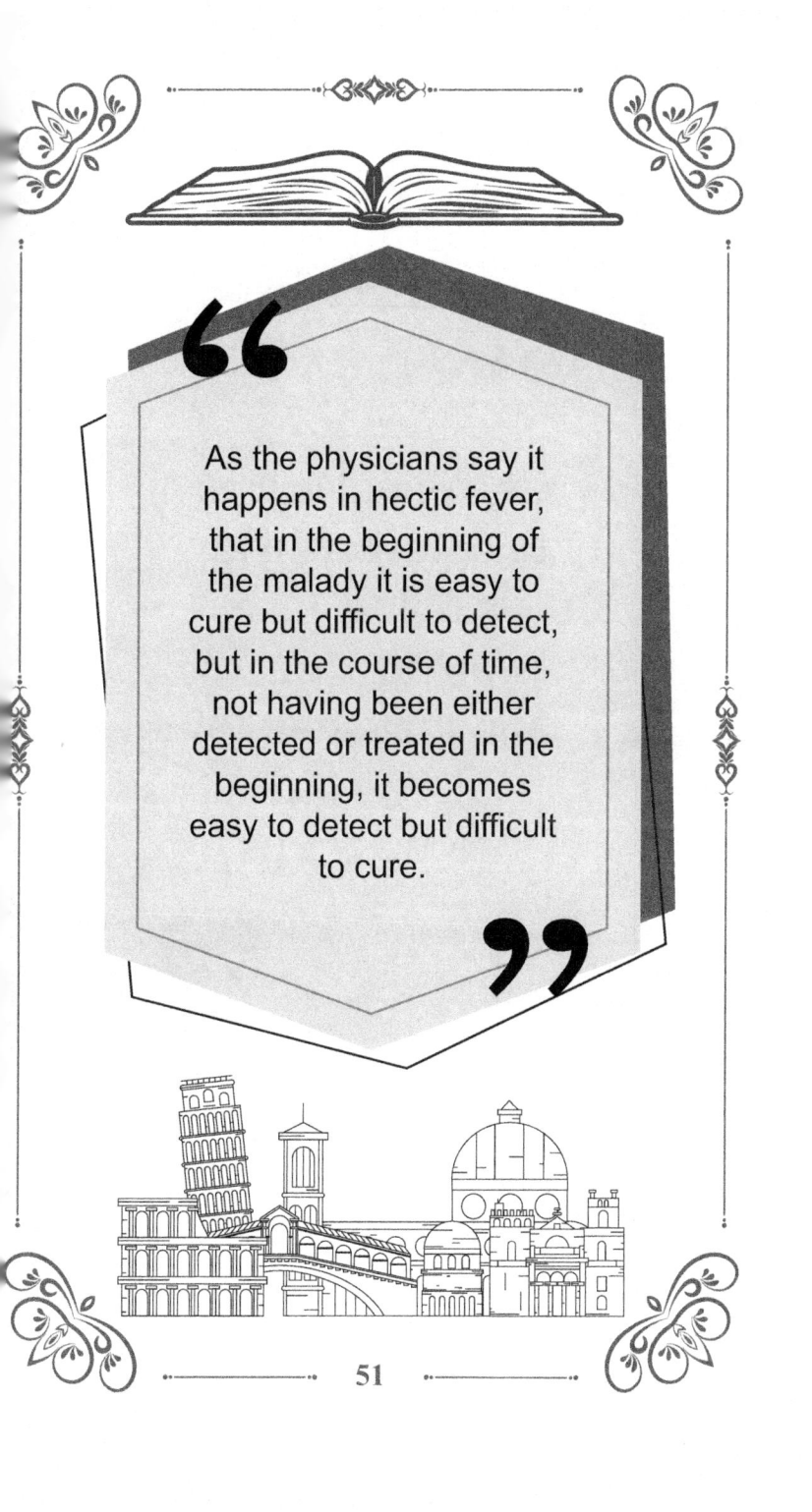

> God is not willing to do everything, and thus take away our free will and that share of glory which belongs to us.

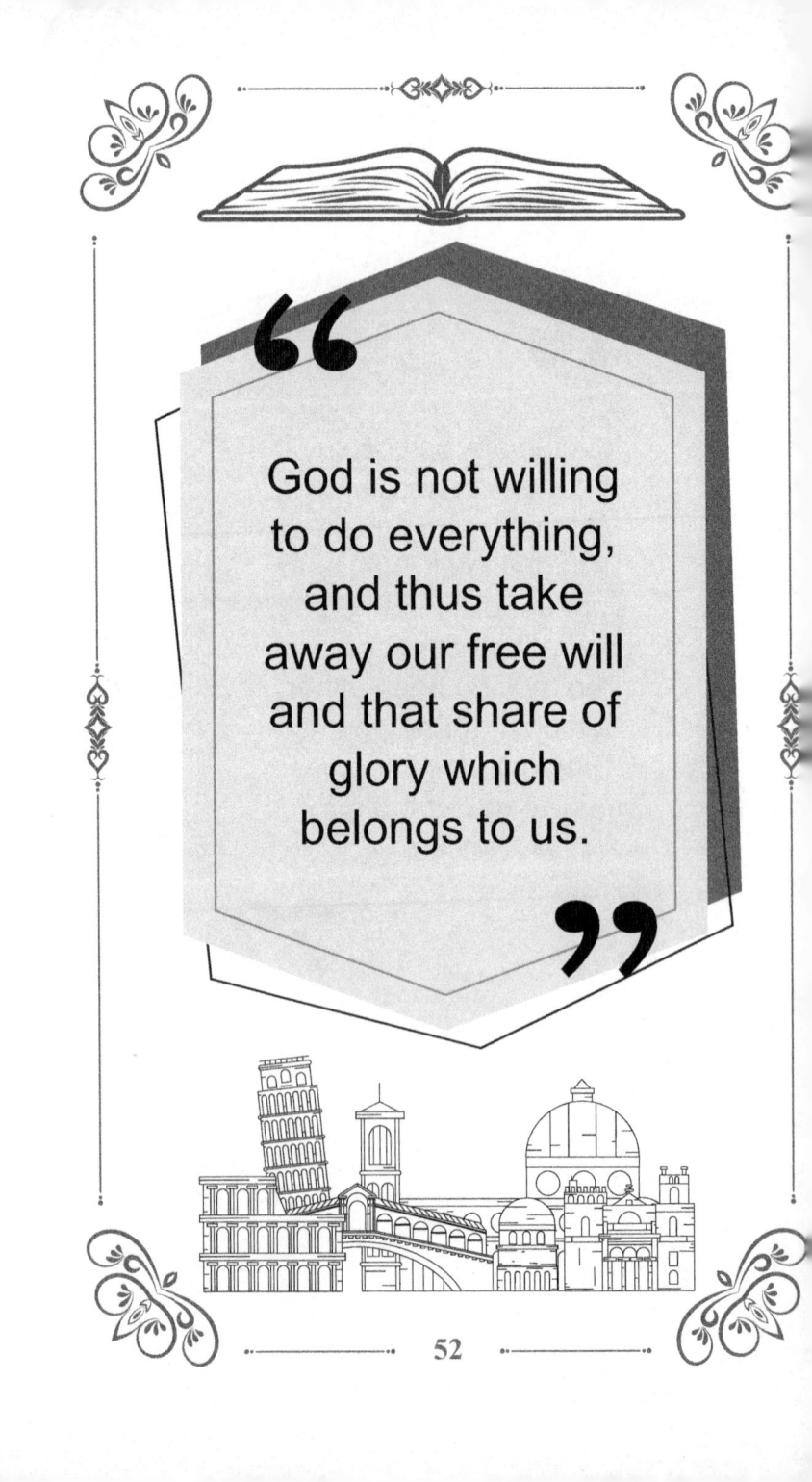

> We have not seen great things done in our time except by those who have been considered mean; the rest have failed.

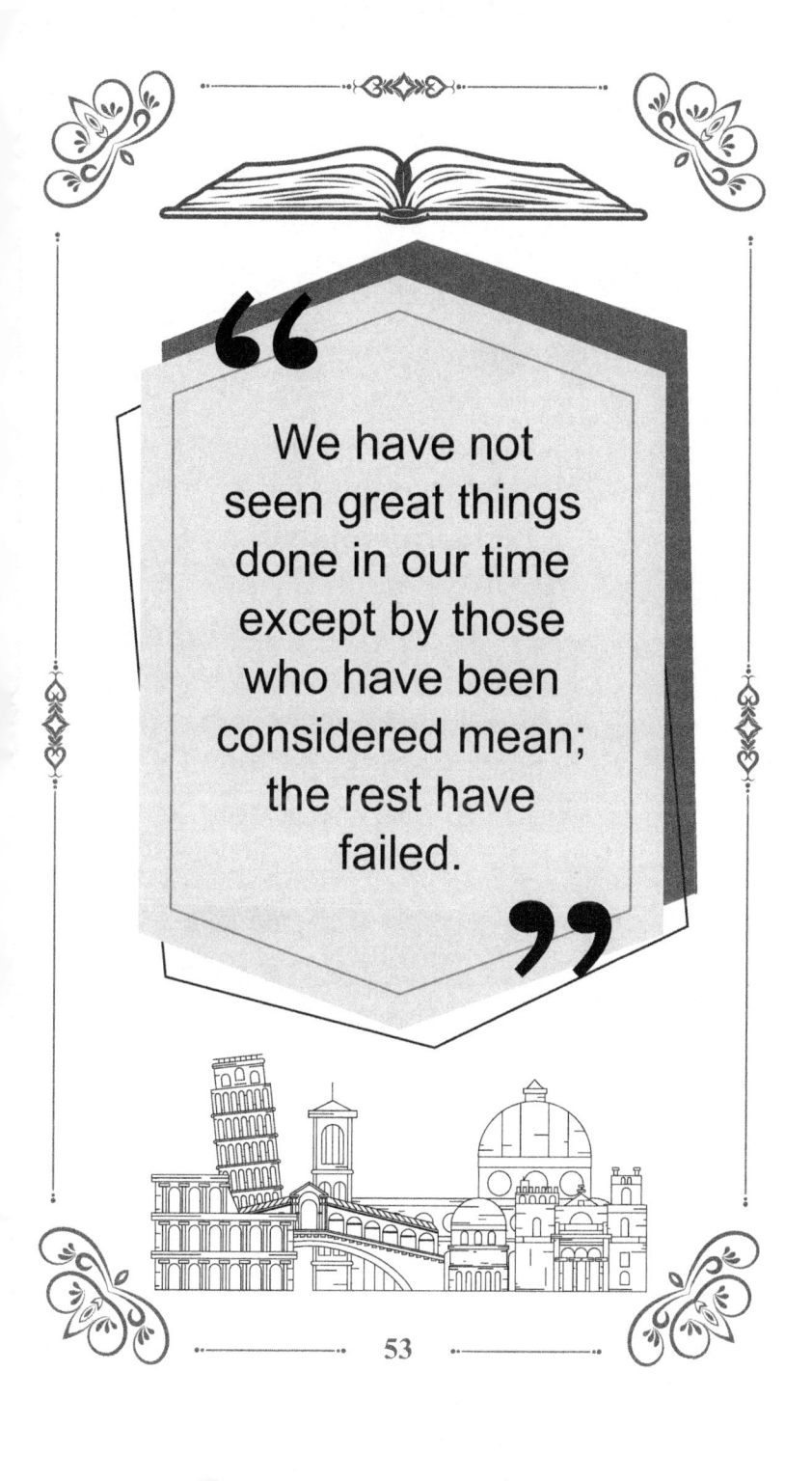

> Occasionally words must serve to veil the facts. But let this happen in such a way that no one become aware of it; or, if it should be noticed, excuses must be at hand to be produced immediately.

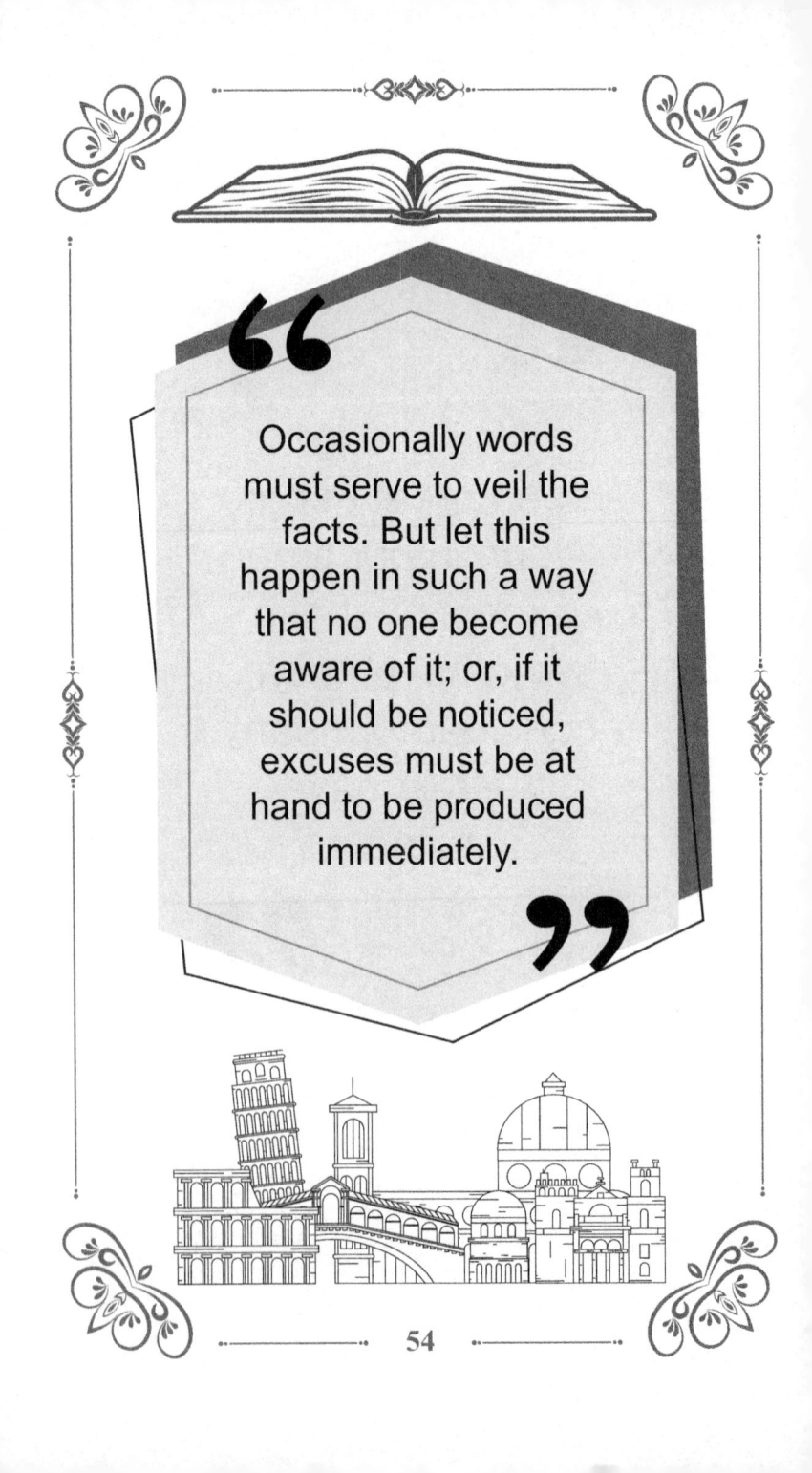

> But in Republics there is a stronger vitality, a fiercer hatred, a keener thirst for revenge. The memory of their former freedom will not let them rest; so that the safest course is either to destroy them, or to go and live in them.

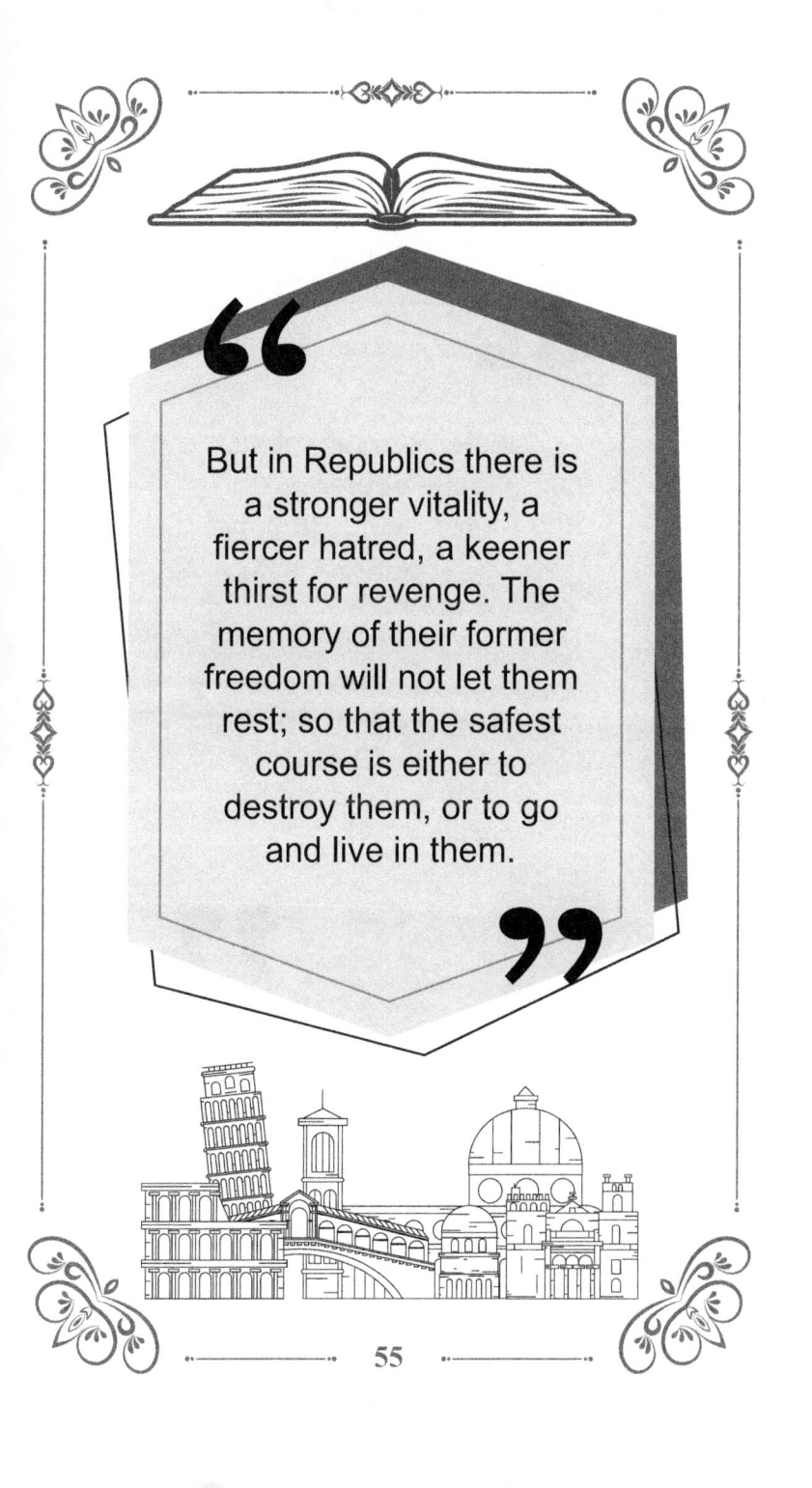

> Women are the most charitable creatures, and the most troublesome. He who shuns women passes up the trouble, but also the benefits. He who puts up with them gains the benefits, but also the trouble. As the saying goes, there's no honey without bees.

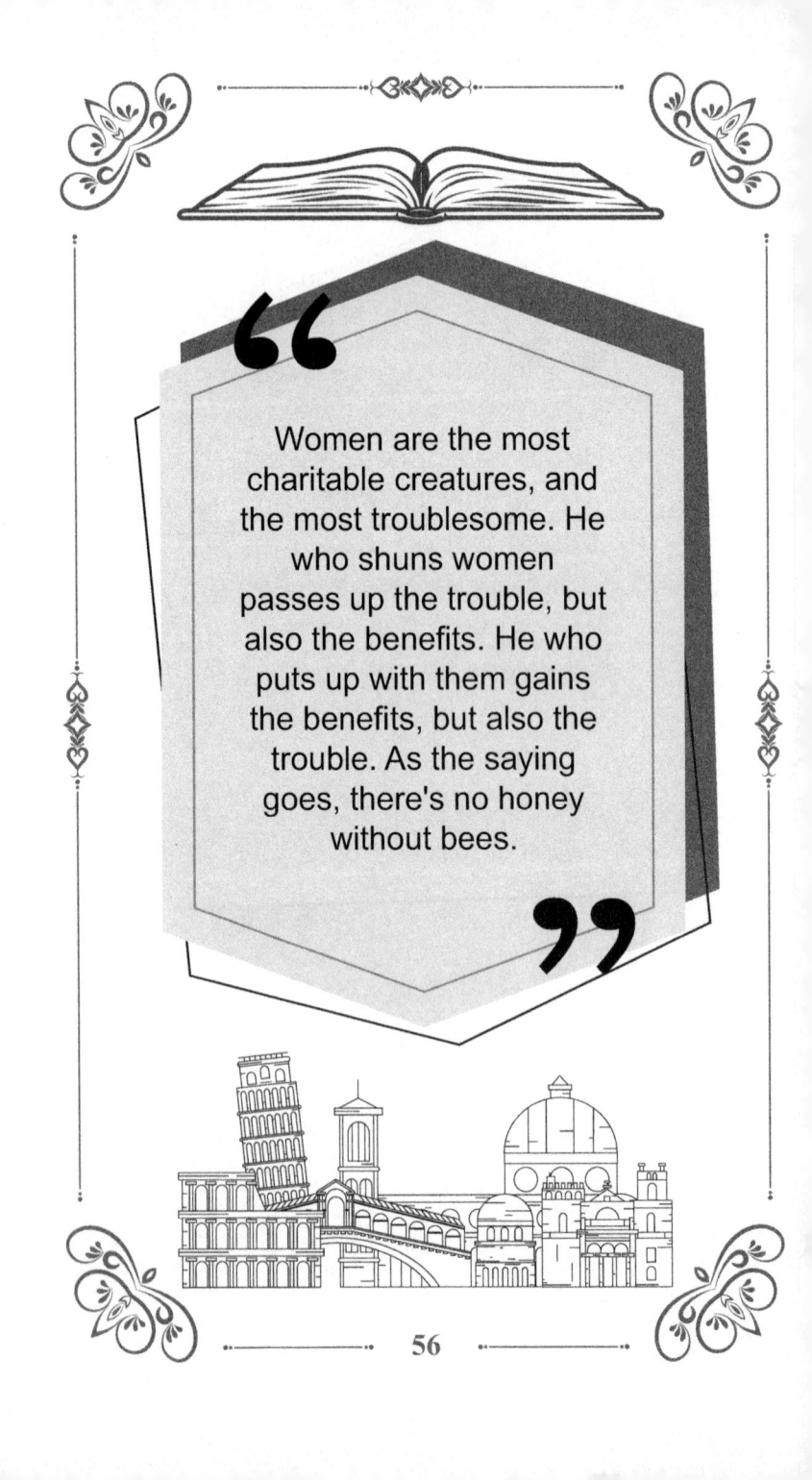

> Alexander never did what he said, Cesare never said what he did.

> In peace one is despoiled by the mercenaries, in war by one's enemies.

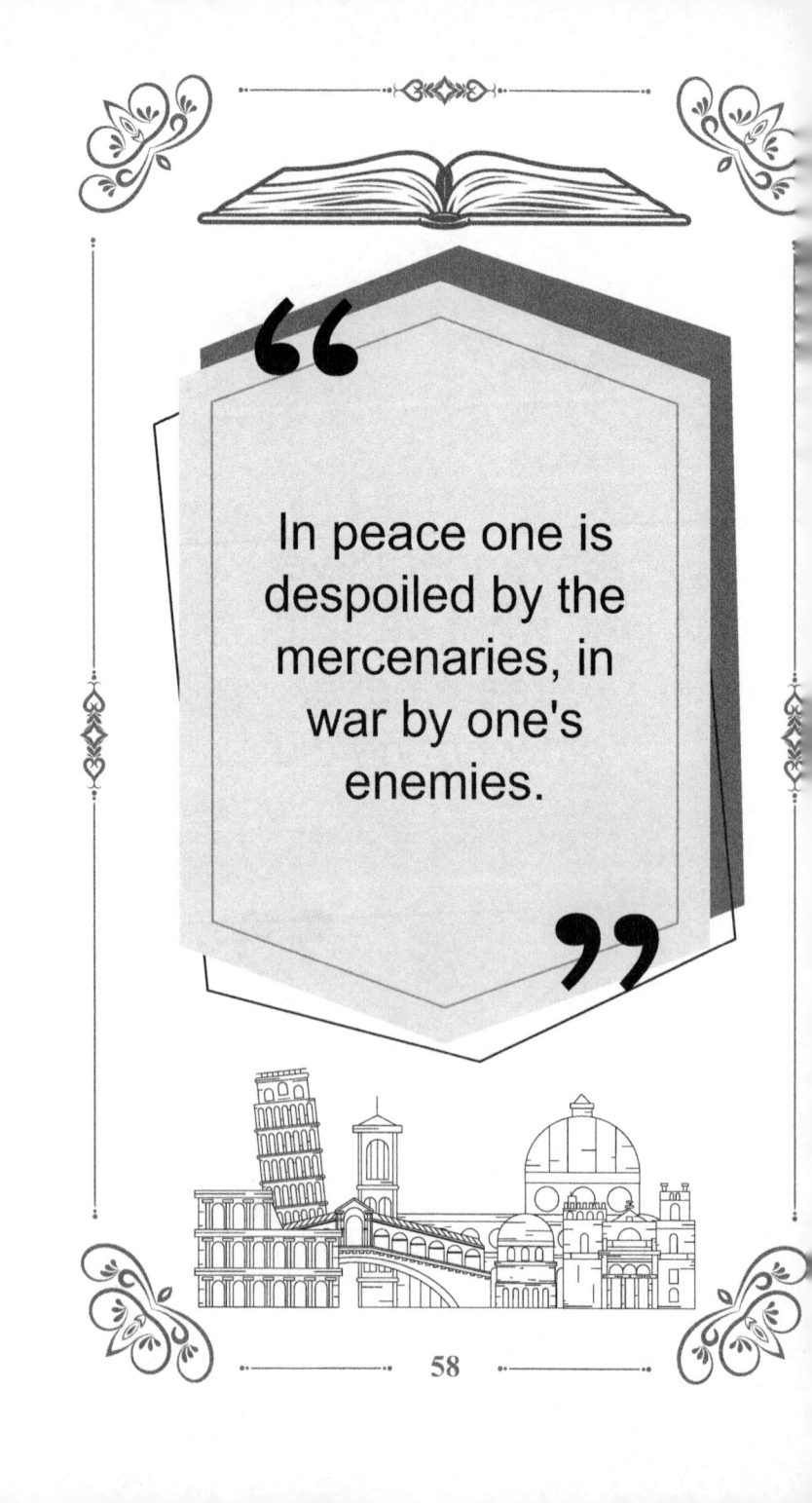

> Men must either be caressed or else destroyed.

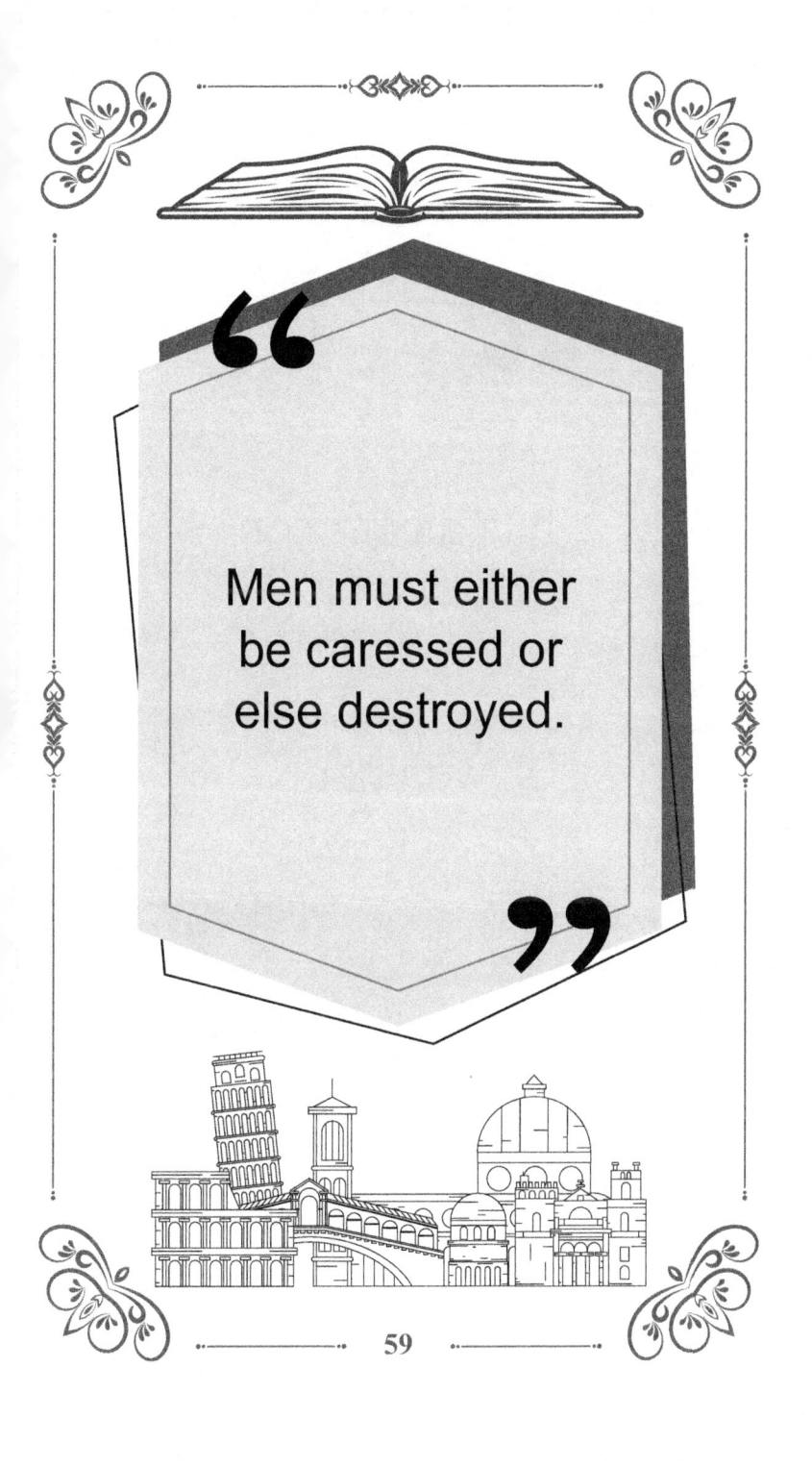

> It is a common fault of men not to reckon on storms in fair weather.

> Let no man, therefore, lose heart from thinking that he cannot do what others have done before him; for, as I said in my Preface, men are born, and live, and die, always in accordance with the same rules.

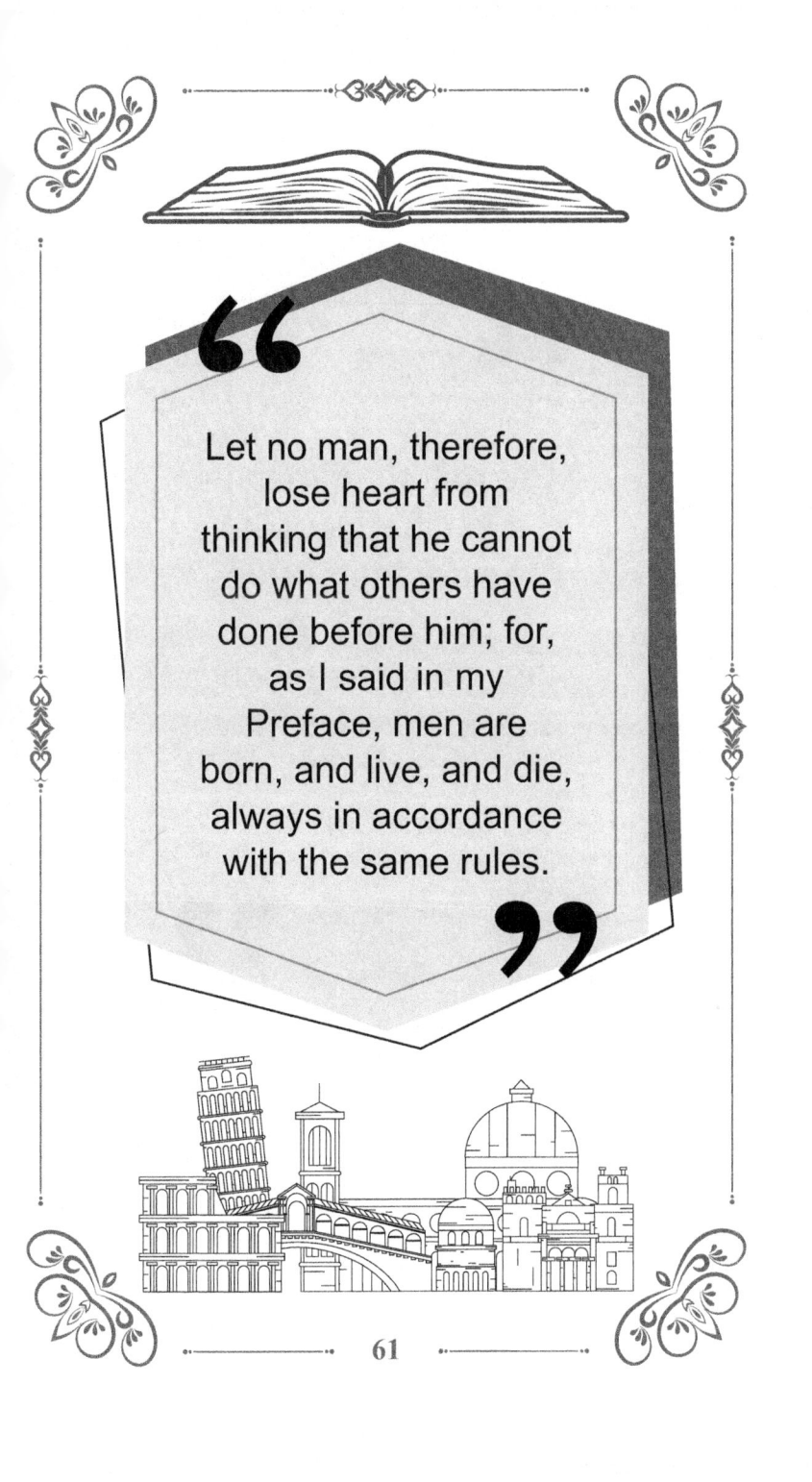

> The nature of man is such that people consider themselves put under an obligation as much by the benefits they confer as by those they receive.

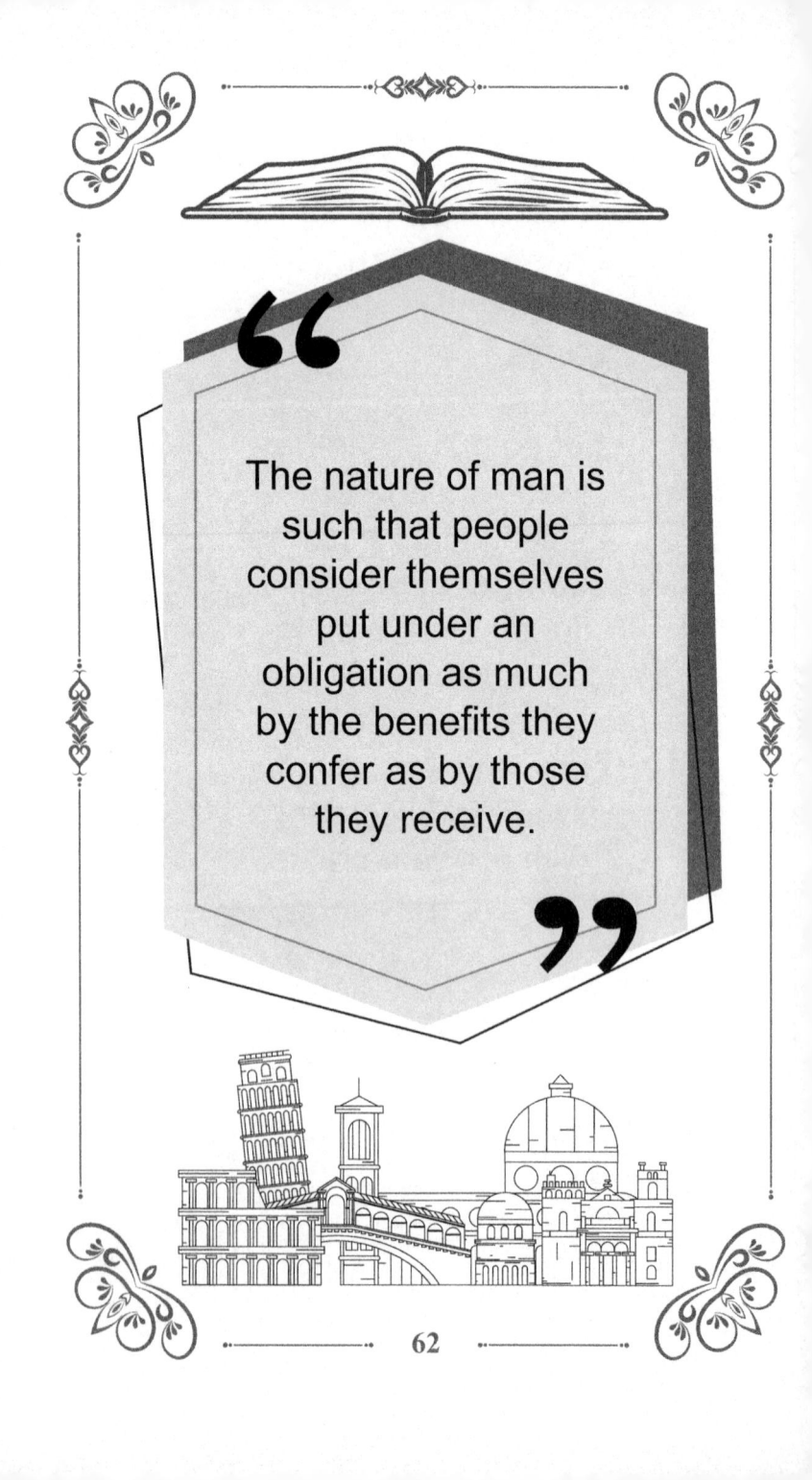

> Never do an enemy a small injury.

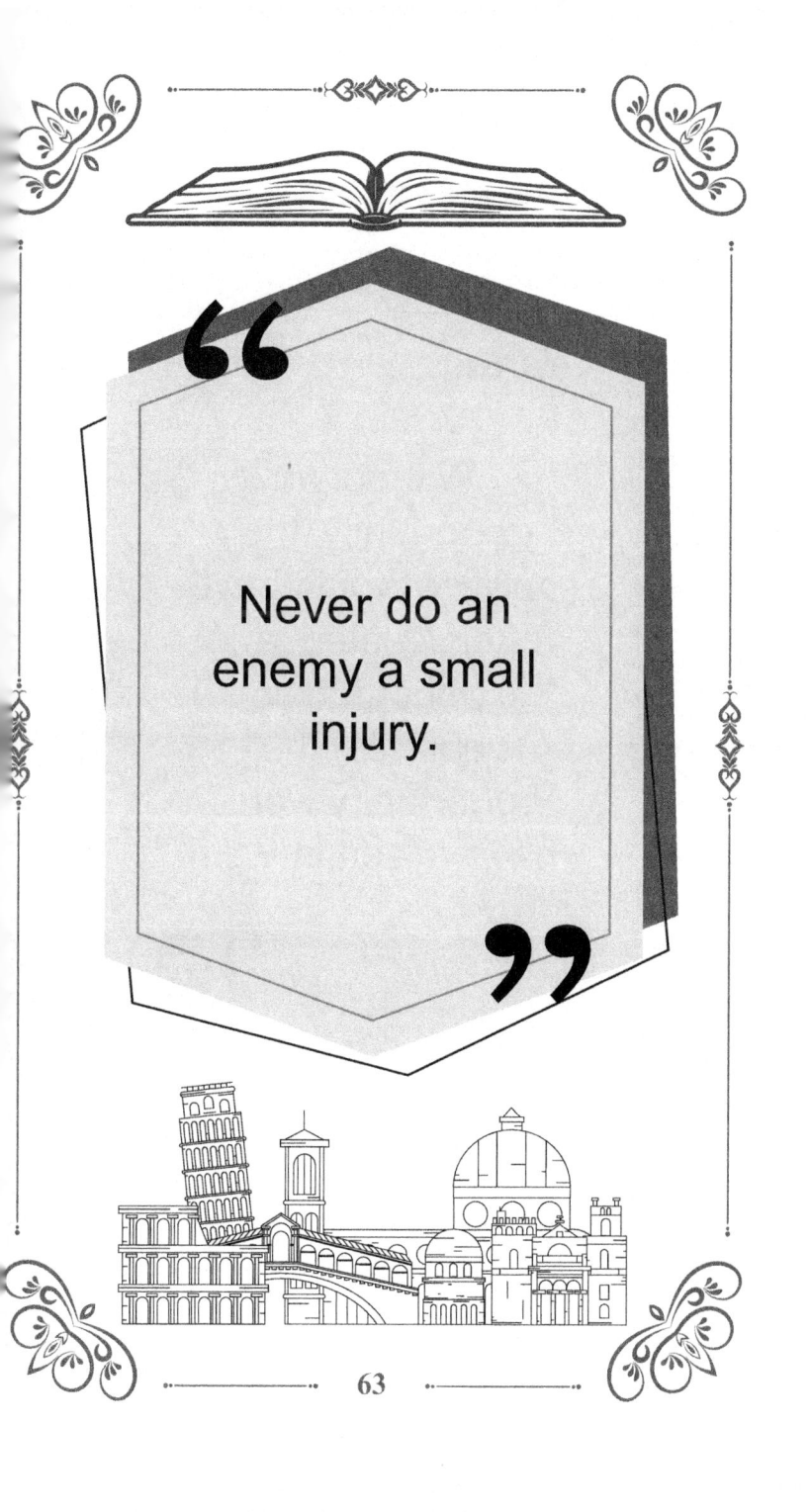

> Without an opportunity, their abilities would have been wasted, and without their abilities, the opportunity would have arisen in vain.

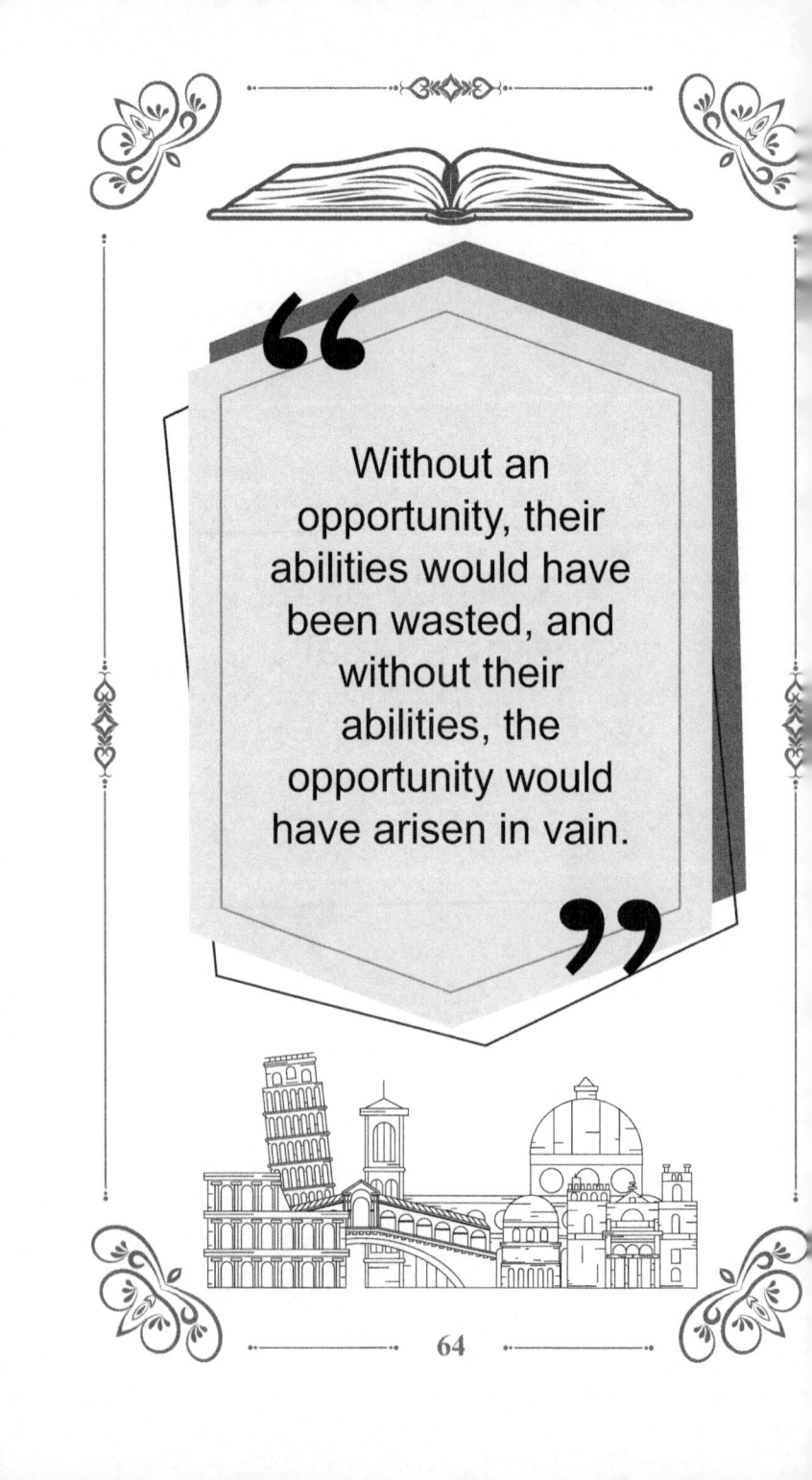

> As a general thing anyone who is not your friend will advise neutrality while anyone who is your friend will ask you to join him, weapon in hand.

> Princes and governments are far more dangerous than other elements within society.

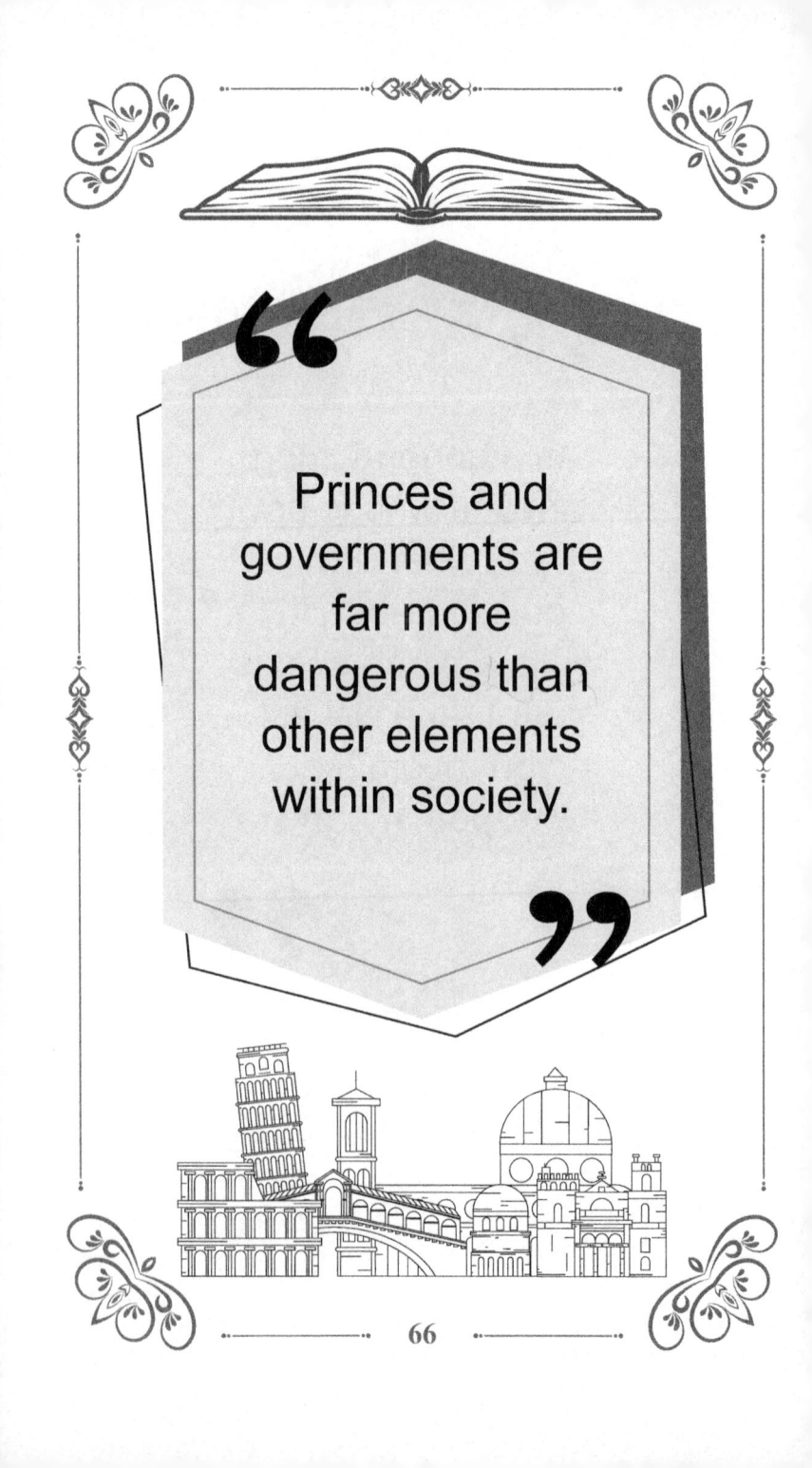

> For however strong you may be in respect of your army, it is essential that in entering a new Province you should have the good will of its inhabitants.

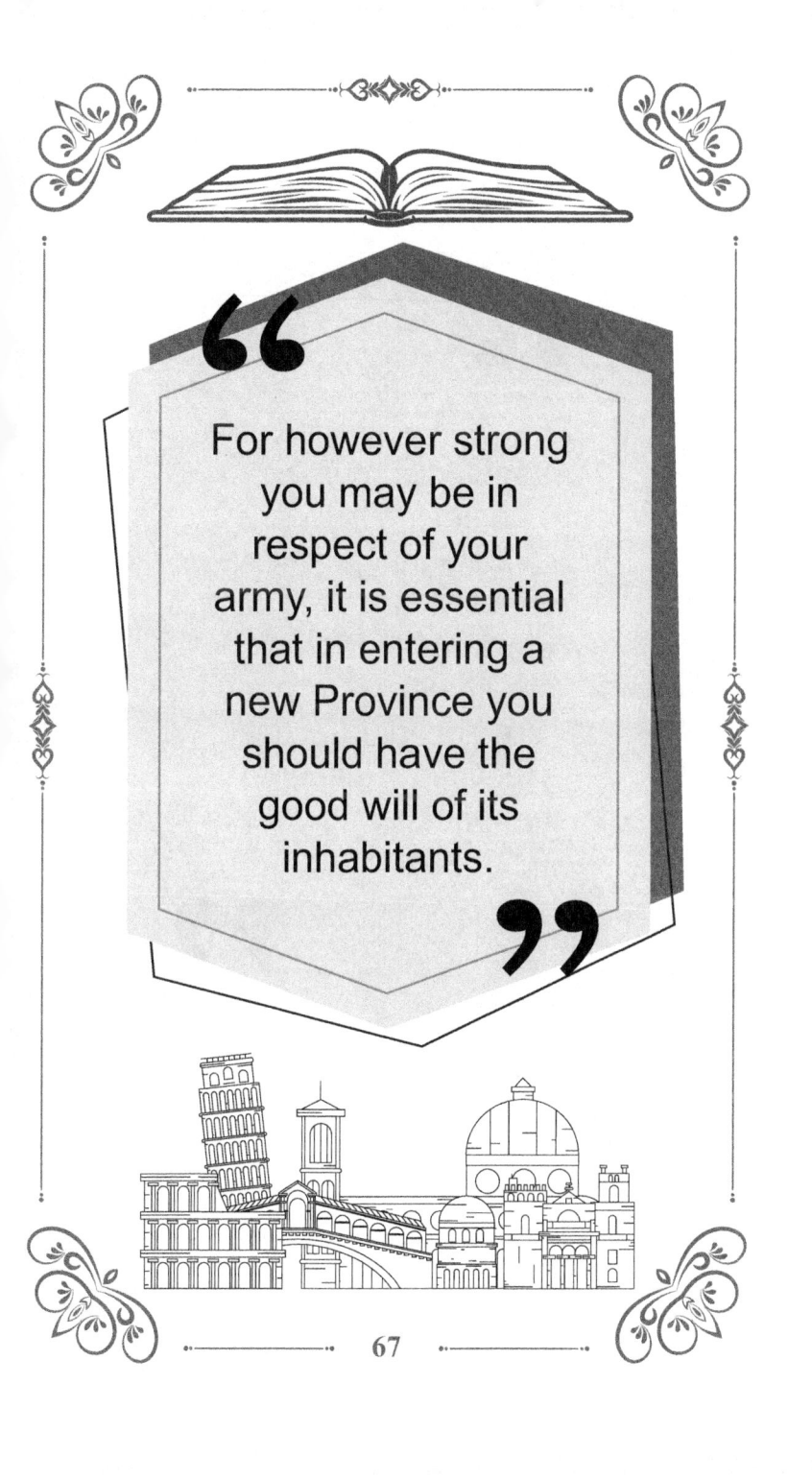

> For when you are on the spot, disorders are detected in their beginnings and remedies can be readily applied; but when you are at a distance, they are not heard of until they have gathered strength and the case is past cure.

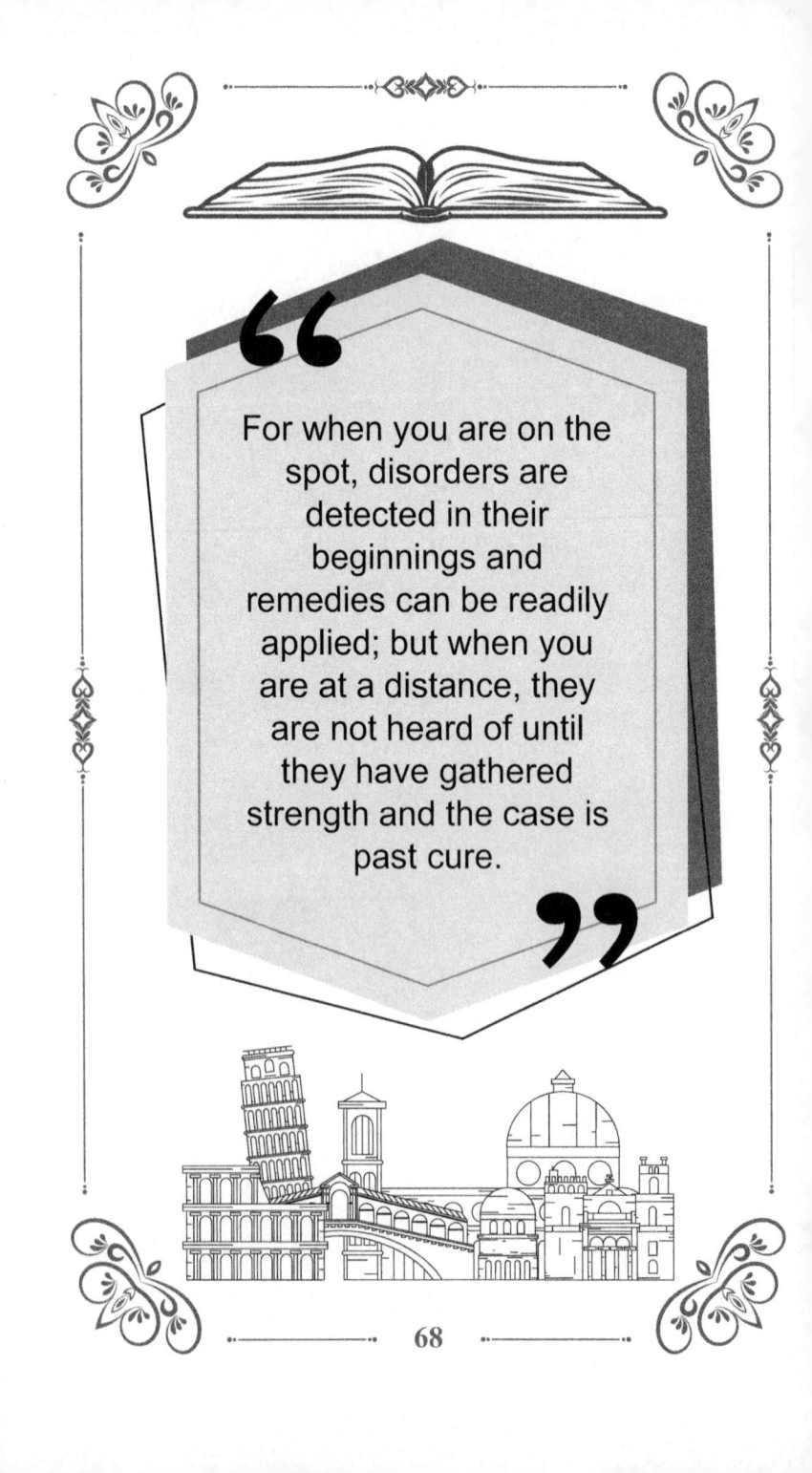

> Whoever desires to found a state and give it laws, must start with assuming that all men are bad and ever ready to display their vicious nature, whenever they may find occasion for it.

> And as the observance of religious teaching is the cause of the greatness of republics, similarly, disdain for it is the cause of their ruin. For where the fear of God is lacking, the state must necessarily either come to ruin or be held together by the fear of a prince that will compensate for the lack of religion.

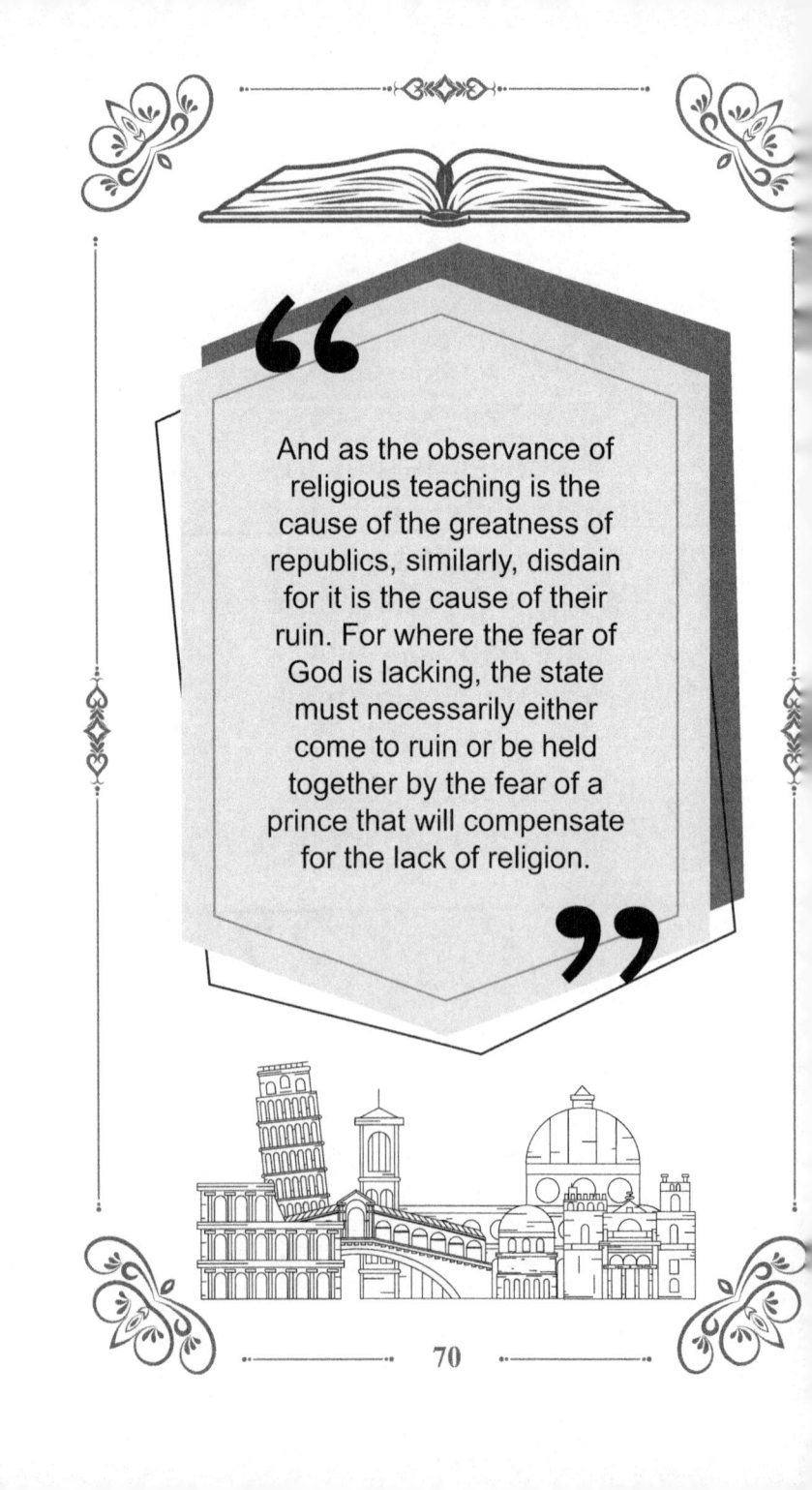

> This is to be asserted in general of men, that they are ungrateful, fickle, false, cowardly, covetous and as long as you succeed they are yours entirely; they will offer you their blood, property, life and children when the need is far distant; but when it approaches they turn against you.

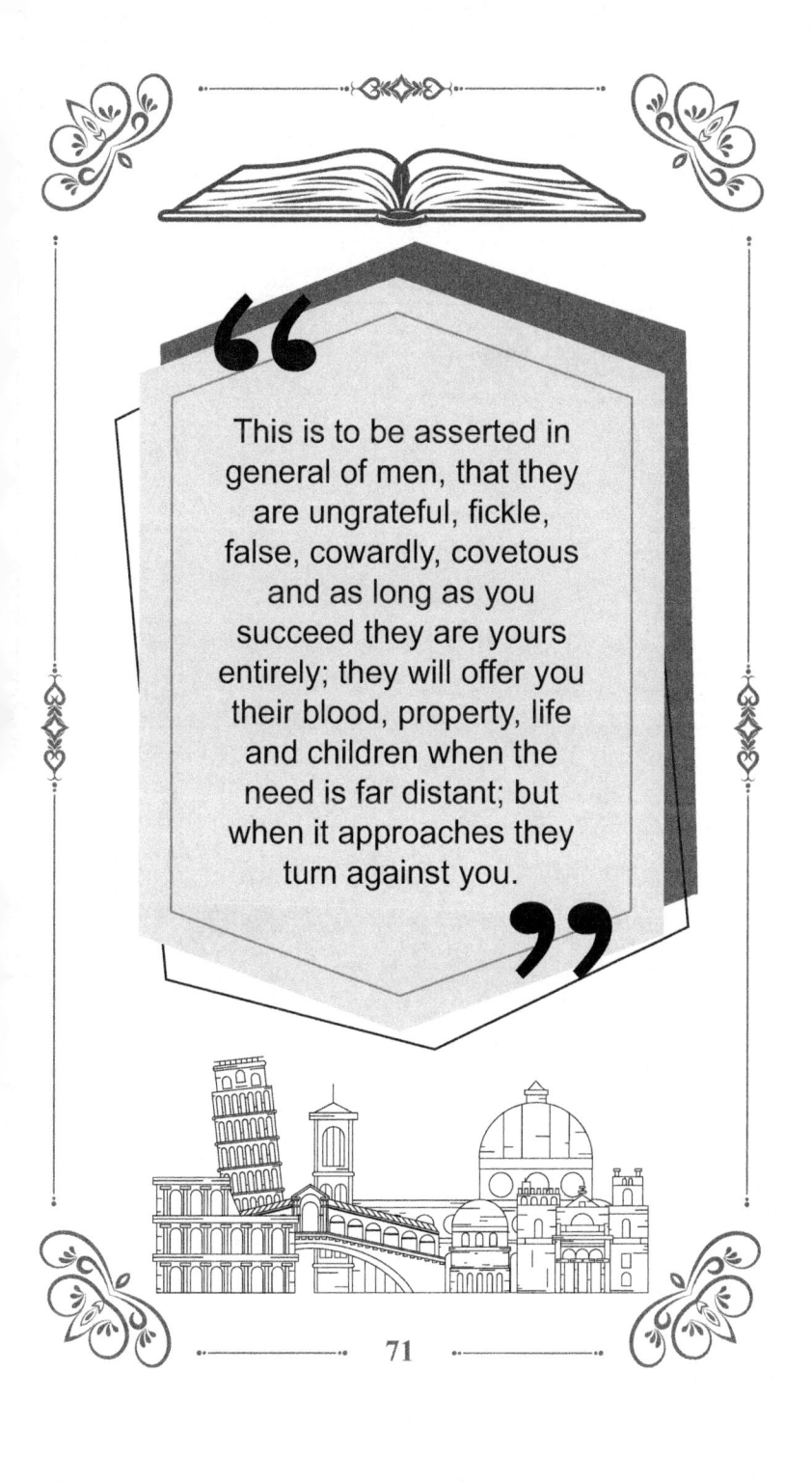

> And he who becomes master of a city accustomed to freedom and does not destroy it may expect to be destroyed by it, for in rebellion it has always the watchword of liberty and its ancient privileges as a rallying point, which neither time nor benefits will ever cause it to forget.

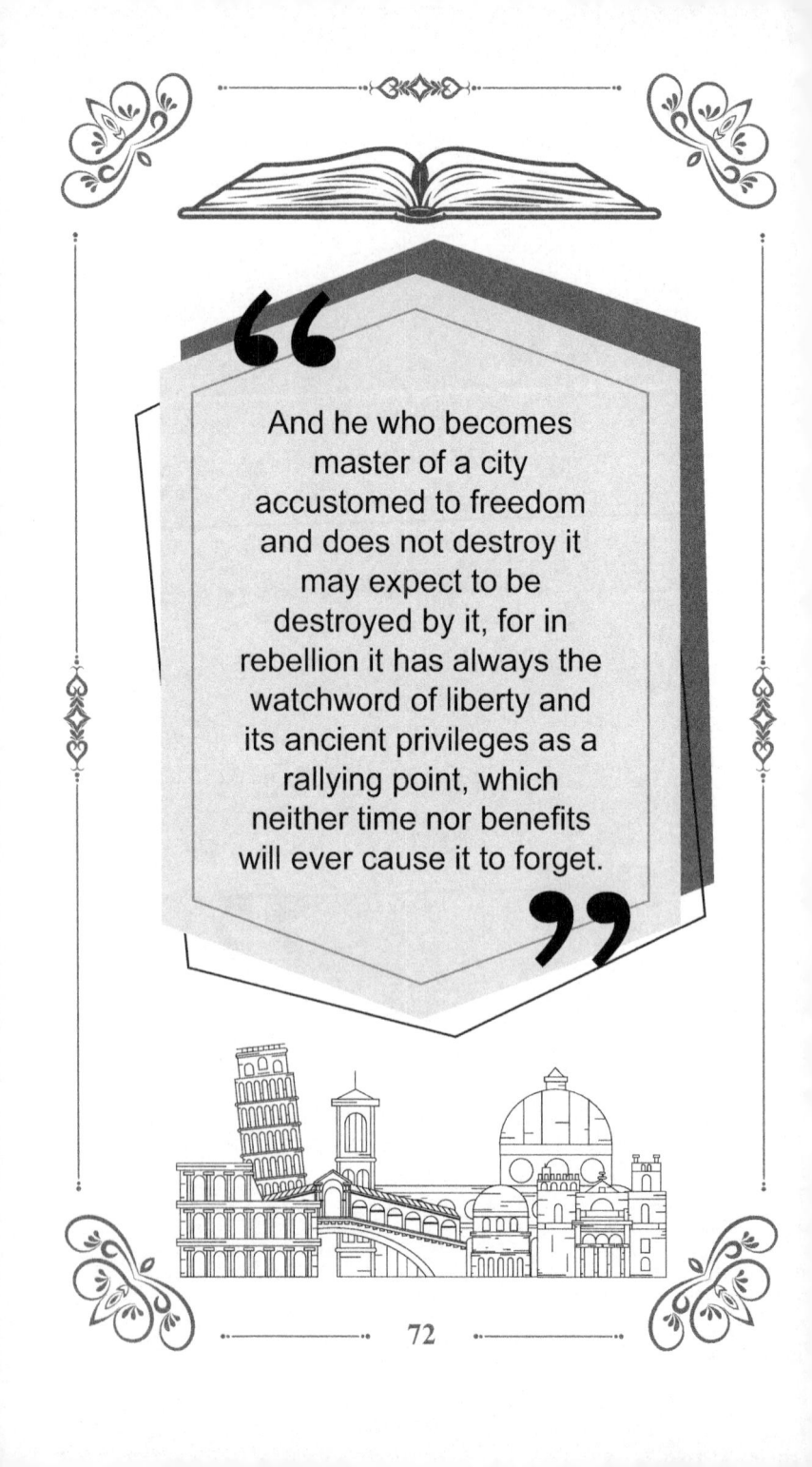

> Though fraud in all other actions be odious, yet in matters of war it is laudable and glorious, and he who overcomes his enemies by stratagem is as much to be praised as he who overcomes them by force.

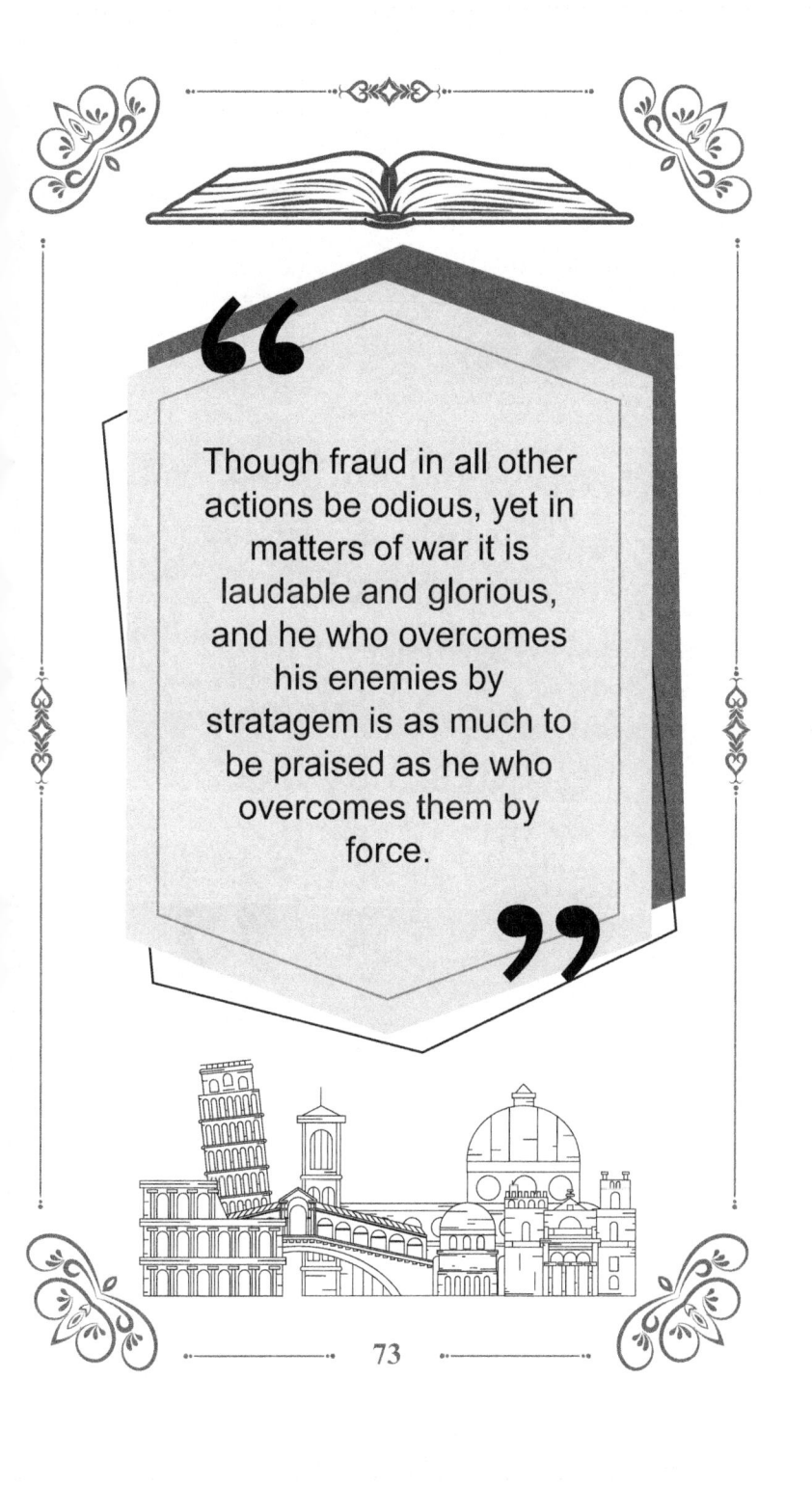

> He who knows that he has not a genius for fighting must learn how to govern by the arts of peace.

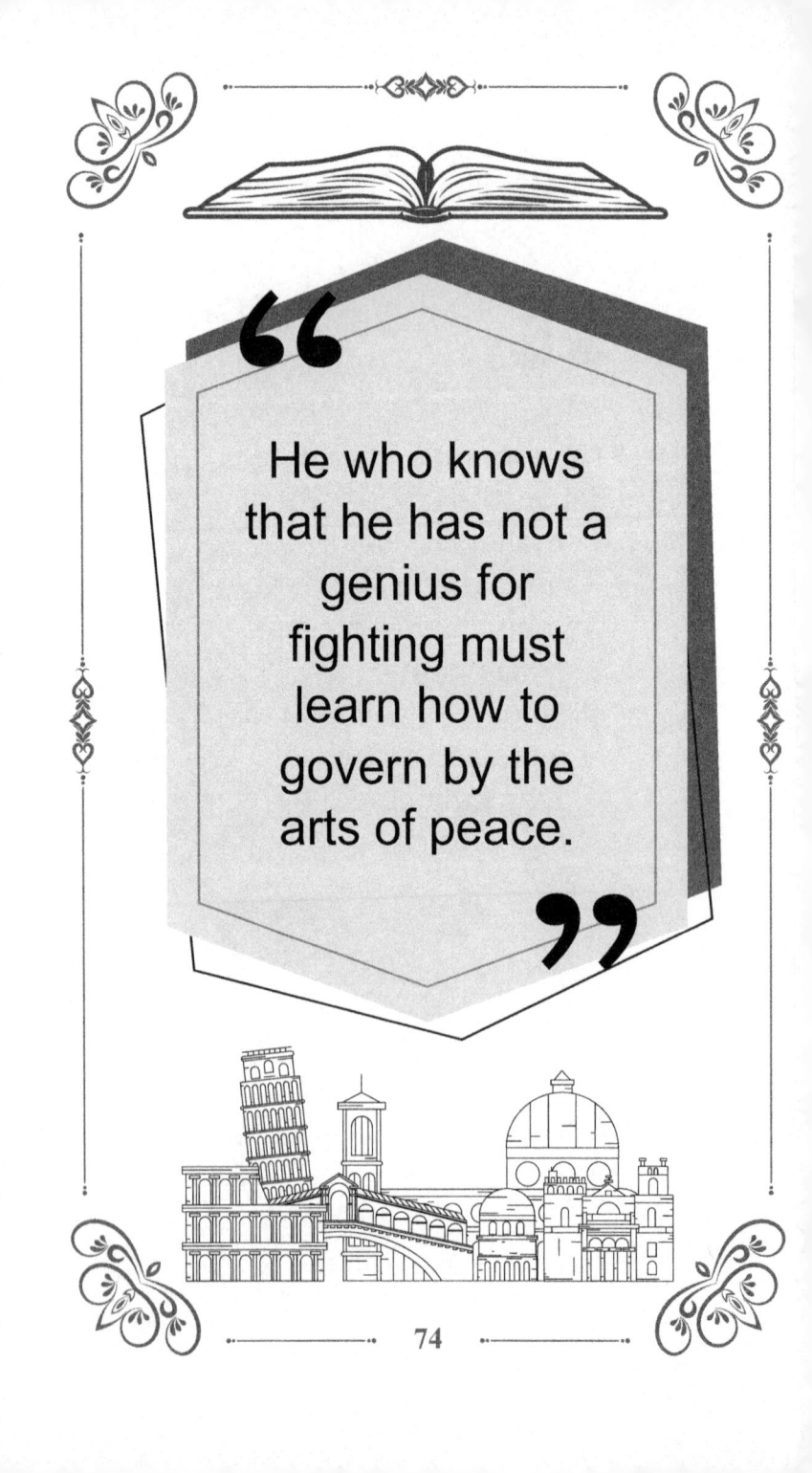

> To defeat Fortune, men must anticipate such evils before they arise, and take prudent steps to avoid them. When the waters have already risen, it is too late to build dikes and embankments.

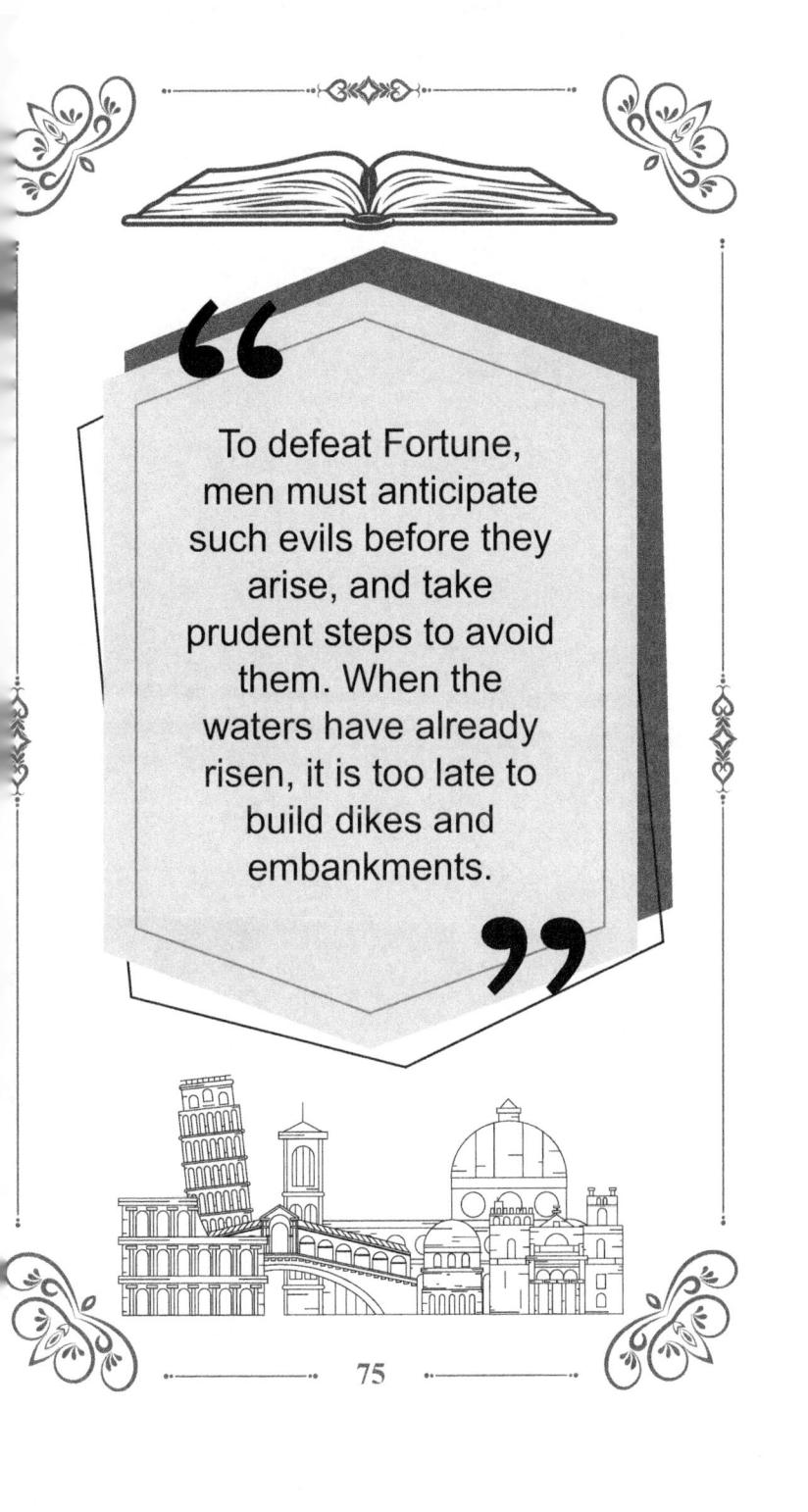

> For a Monarchy readily becomes a Tyranny, an Aristocracy an Oligarchy, while a Democracy tends to degenerate into Anarchy.

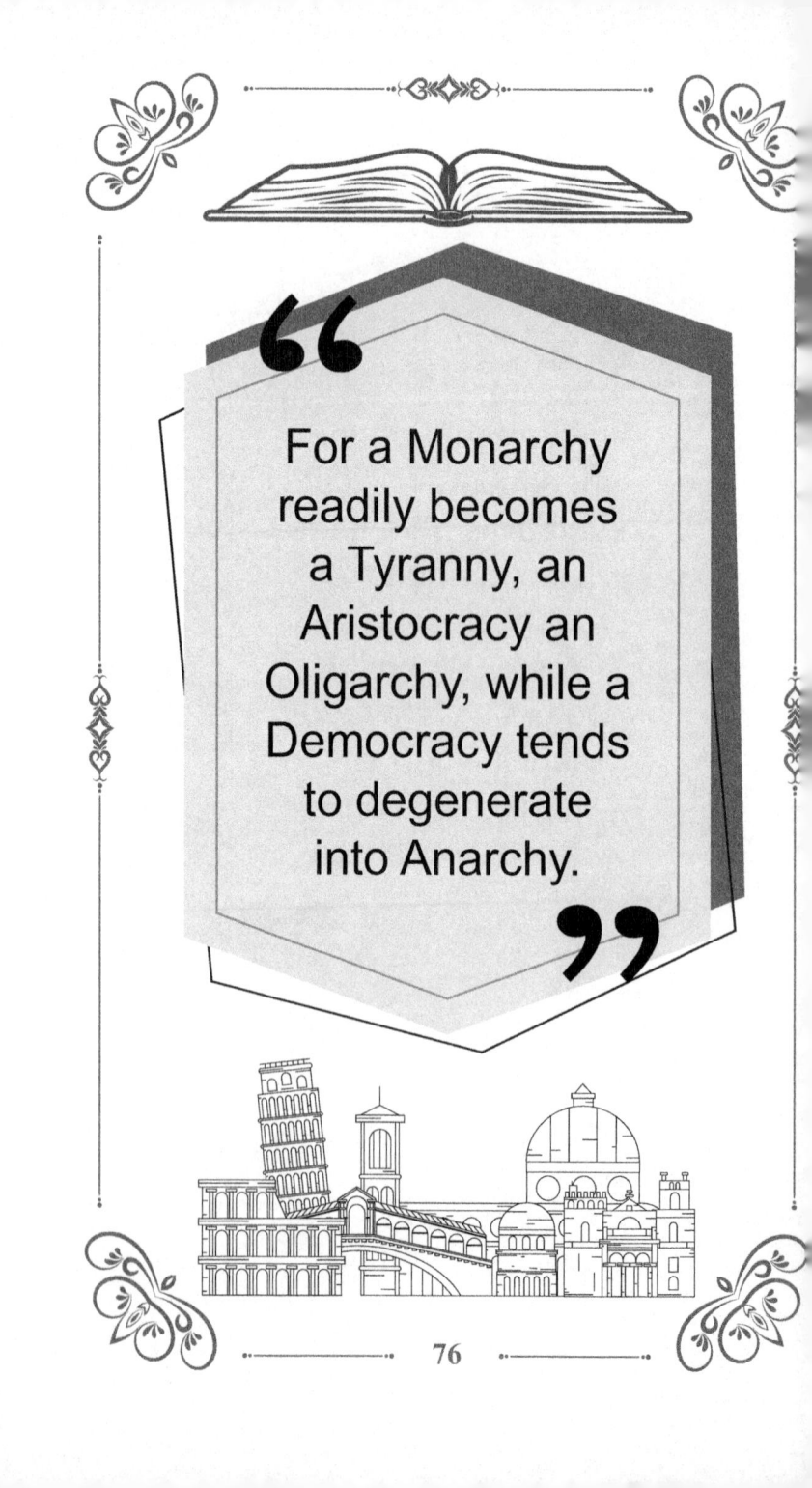

> Men live peacefully as long as their old way of life is maintained and there is no change in customs.

> I hold strongly to this: that it is better to be impetuous than circumspect; because fortune is a woman and if she is to be submissive it is necessary to beat and coerce her.

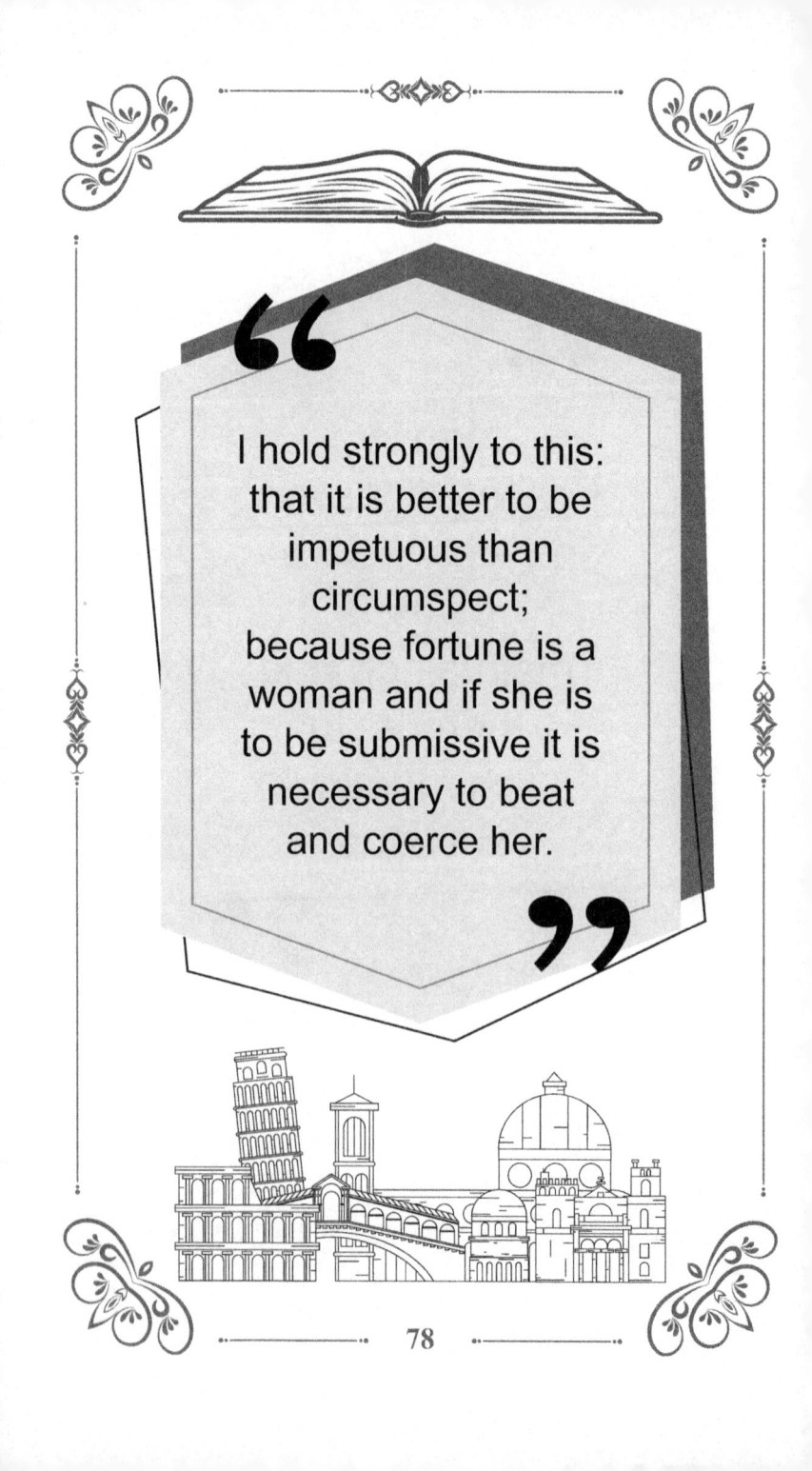

> Hence it comes that all armed prophets have been victorious, and all unarmed prophets have been destroyed.

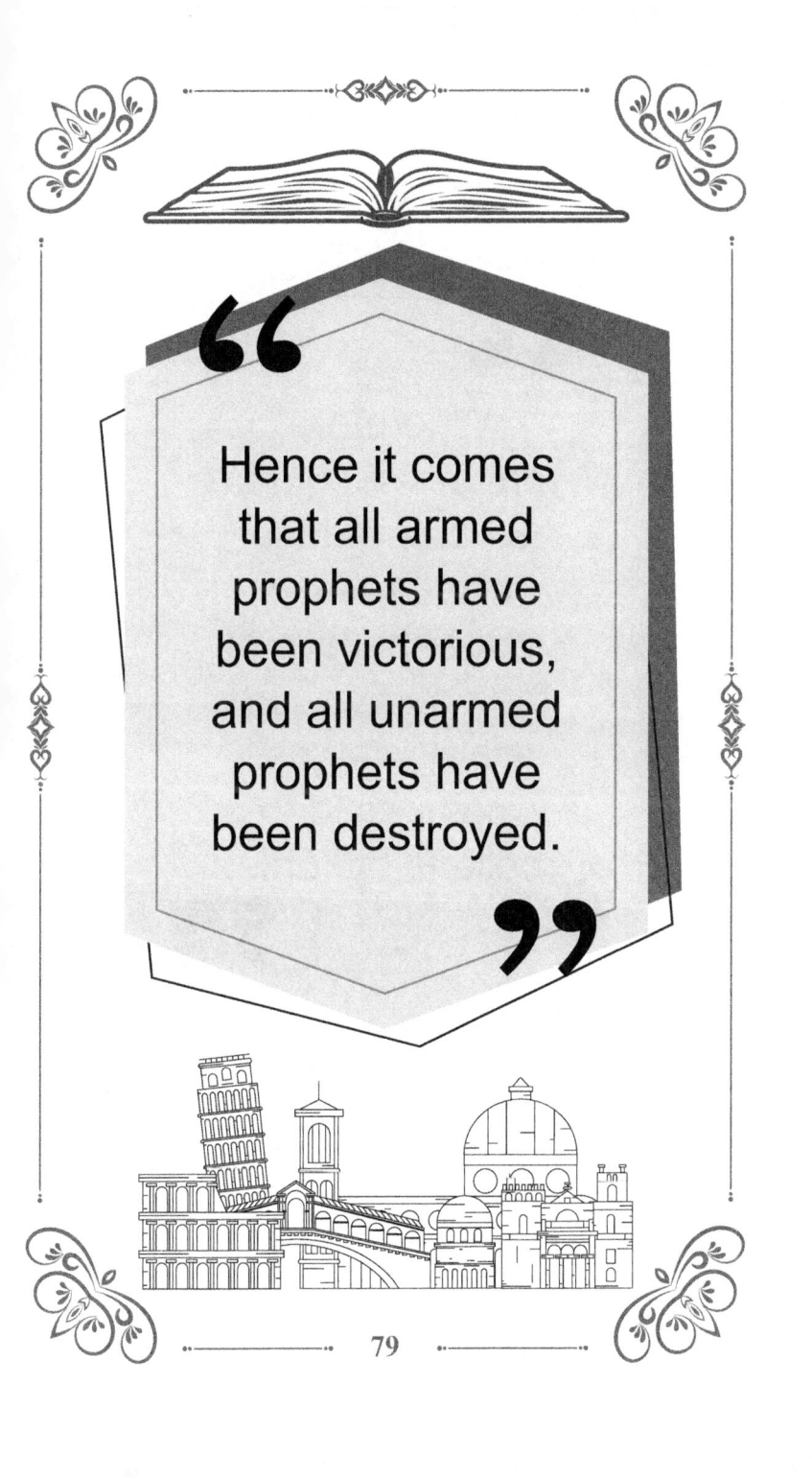

> Wherefore, matters should be so ordered that when men no longer believe of their own accord, they may be compelled to believe by force.

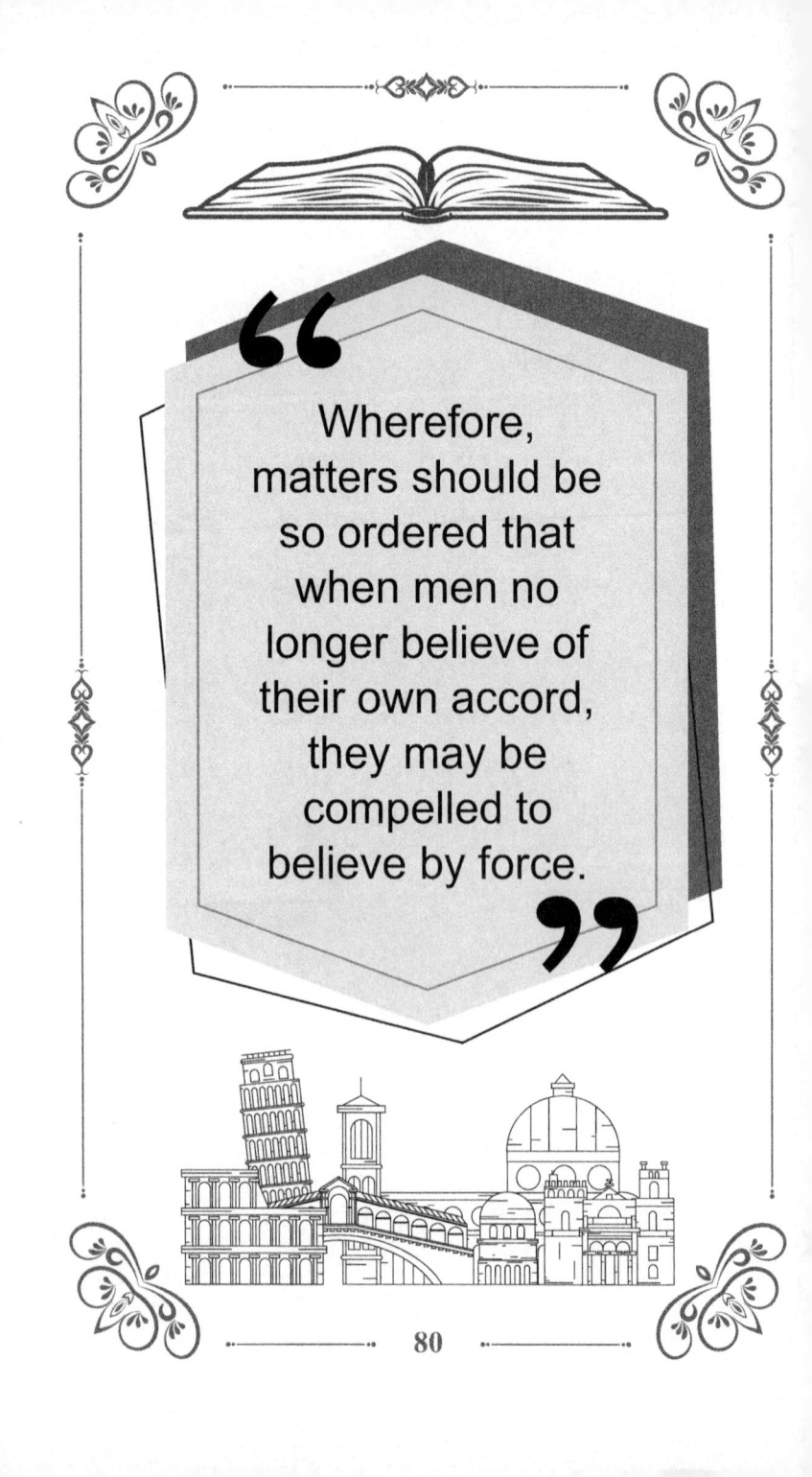

> No enterprise is more likely to succeed than one concealed from the enemy until it is ripe for execution.

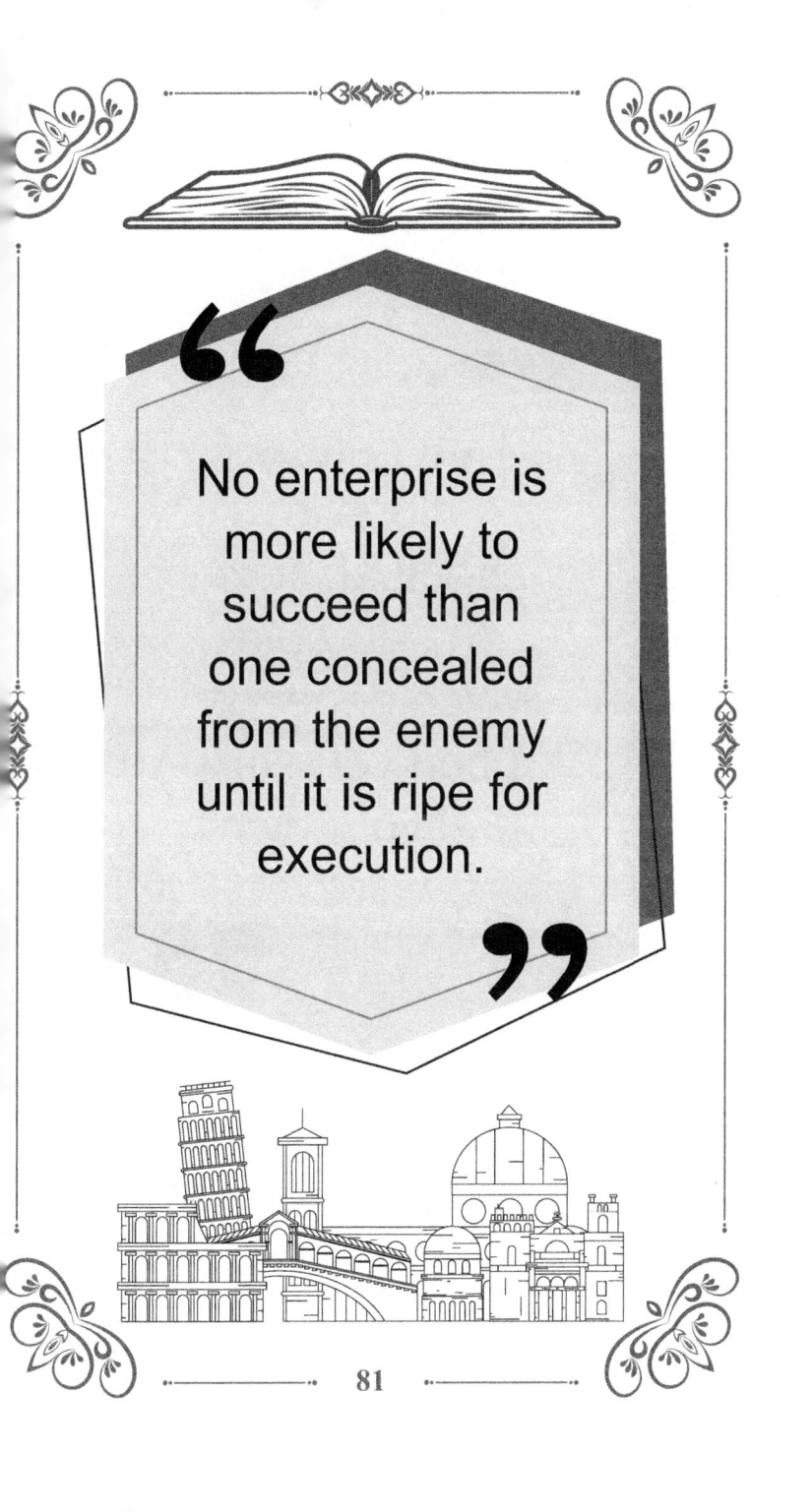

> That defense alone is effectual, sure and durable which depends upon yourself and your own valor.

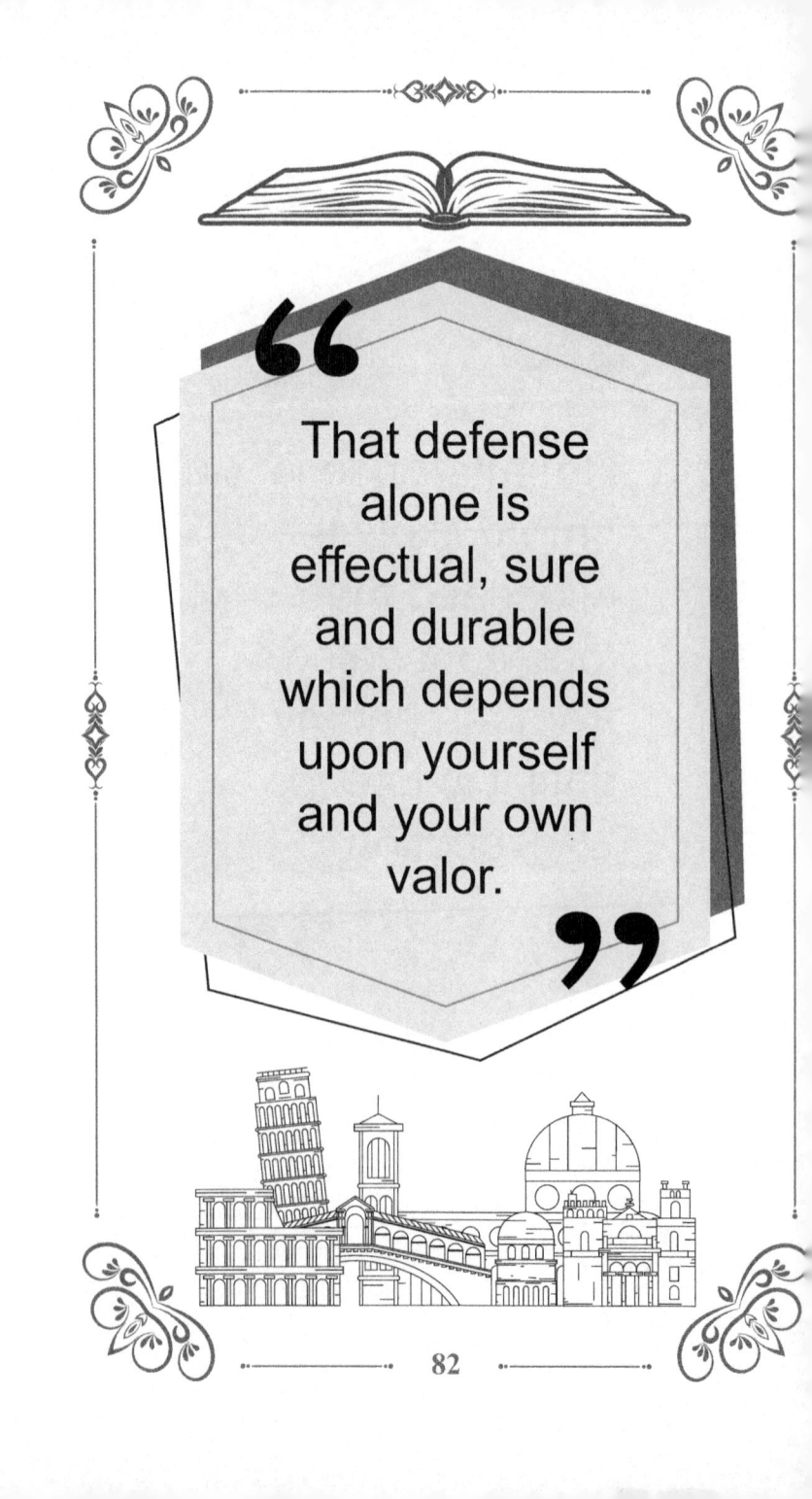

> For Time, driving all things before it, may bring with it evil as well as good.

> The people, as Cicero says, may be ignorant, but they can recognize the truth and will readily yield when some trustworthy man explains it to them.

> For the friendships which we buy with a price, and do not gain by greatness and nobility of character, though they be fairly earned are not made good, but fail us when we have occasion to use them.

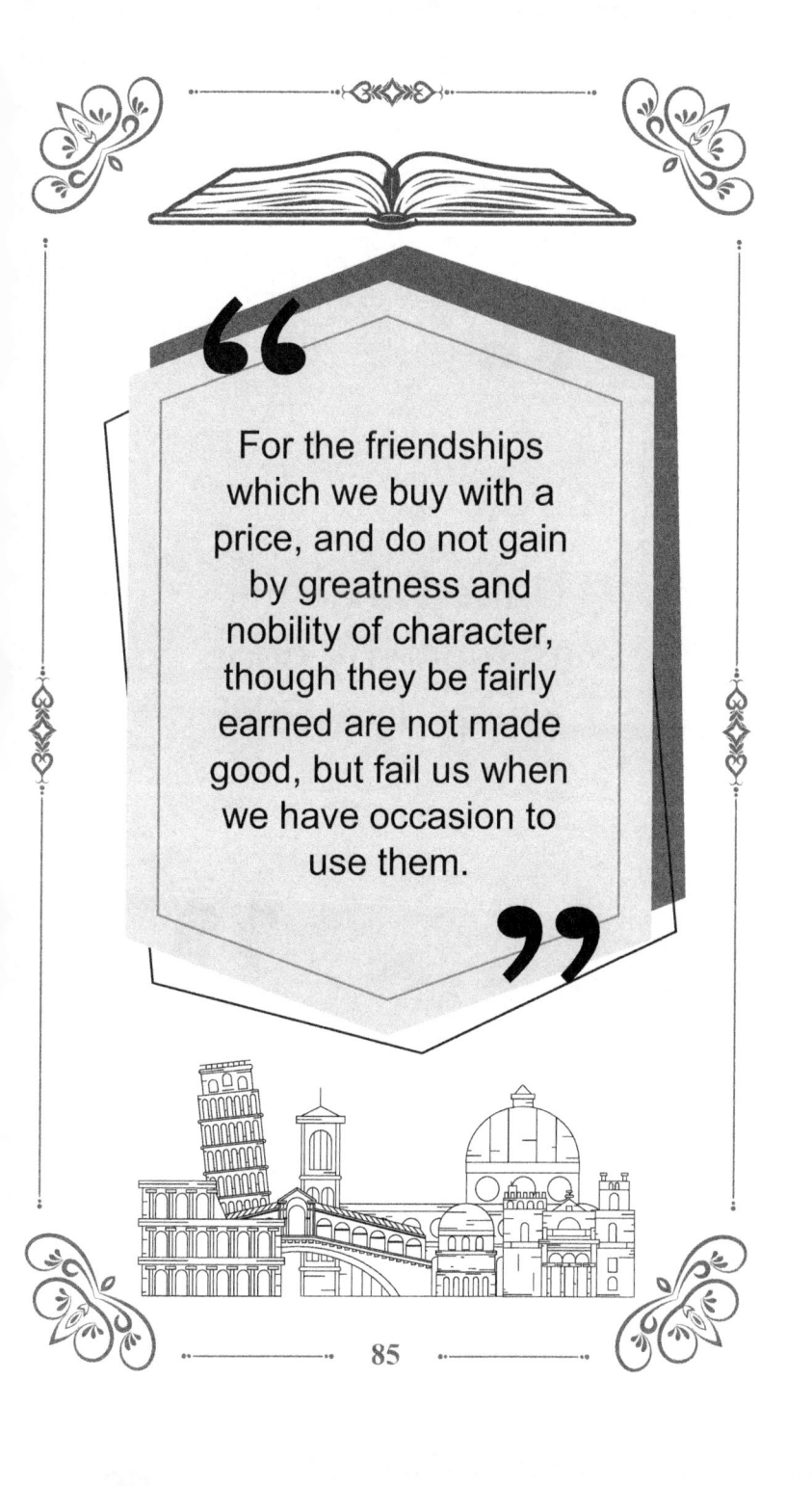

> Hatred is gained as much by good works as by evil.

> A people accustomed to live under a prince, if by any accident it becomes free, finds it difficult to maintain its liberty.

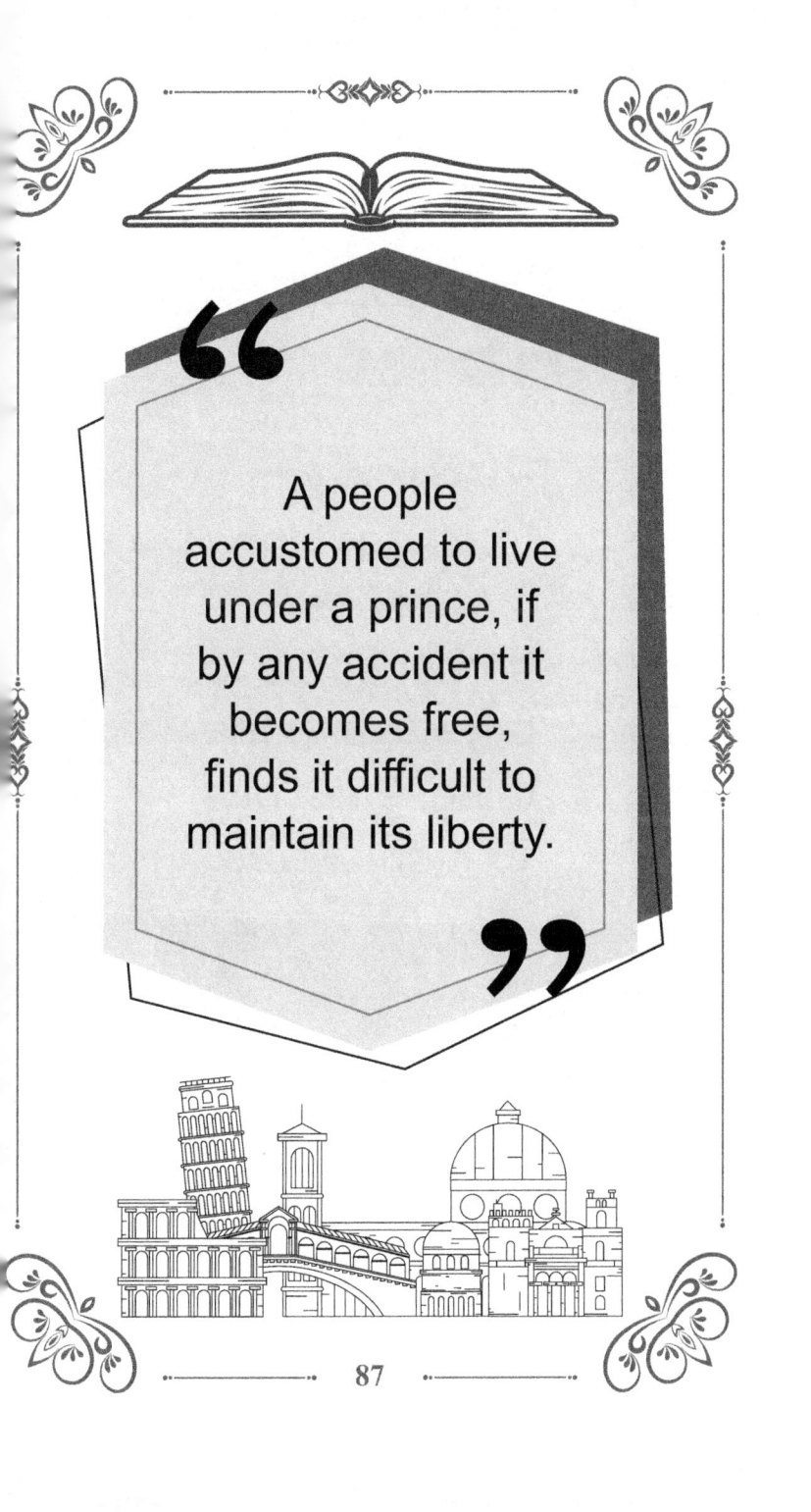

> Princes ought to delegate the things burdensome to others, and the things gracious to themselves.

> Wars begin when you will, but they do not end when you please.

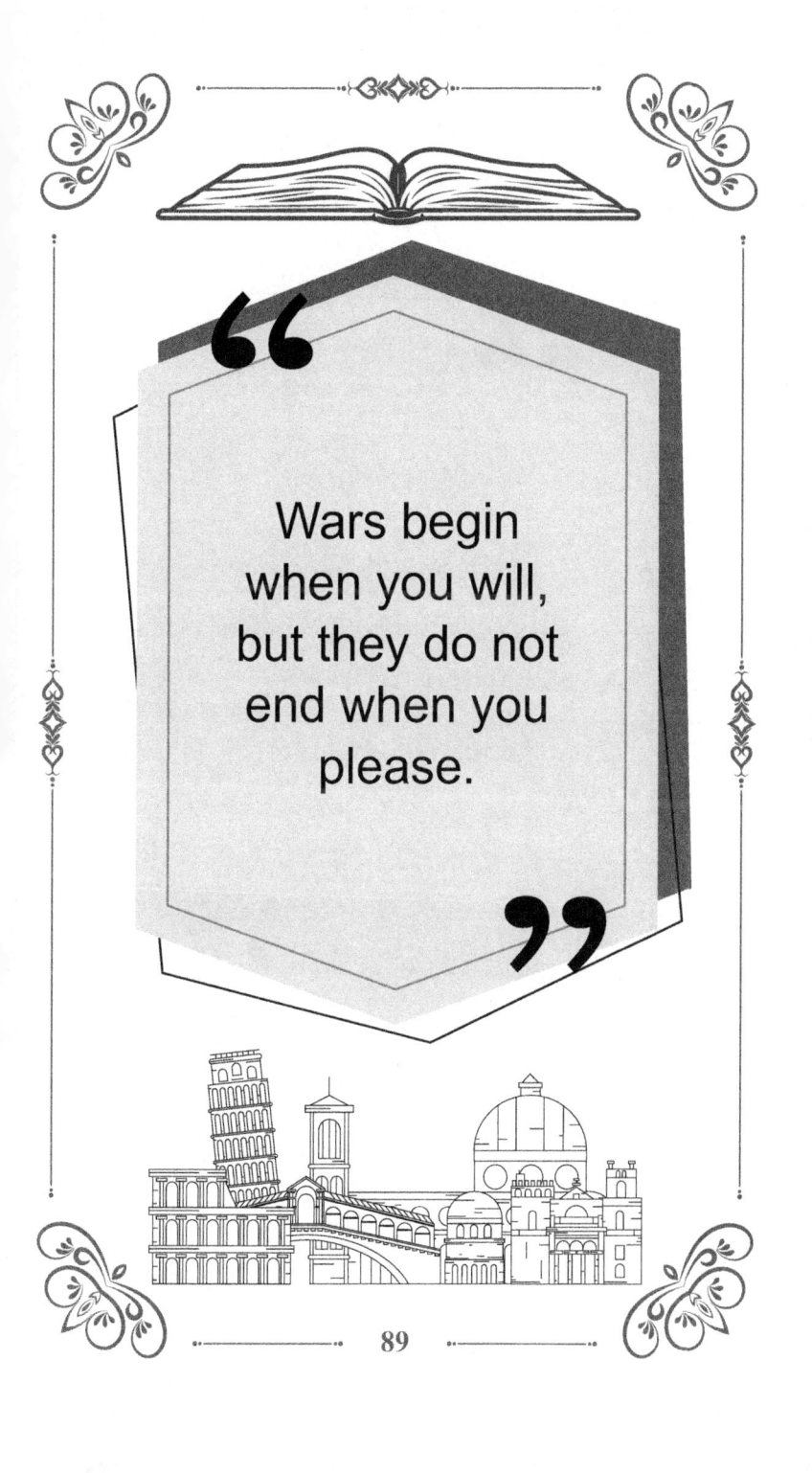

> The vulgar are always taken by what a thing seems to be.

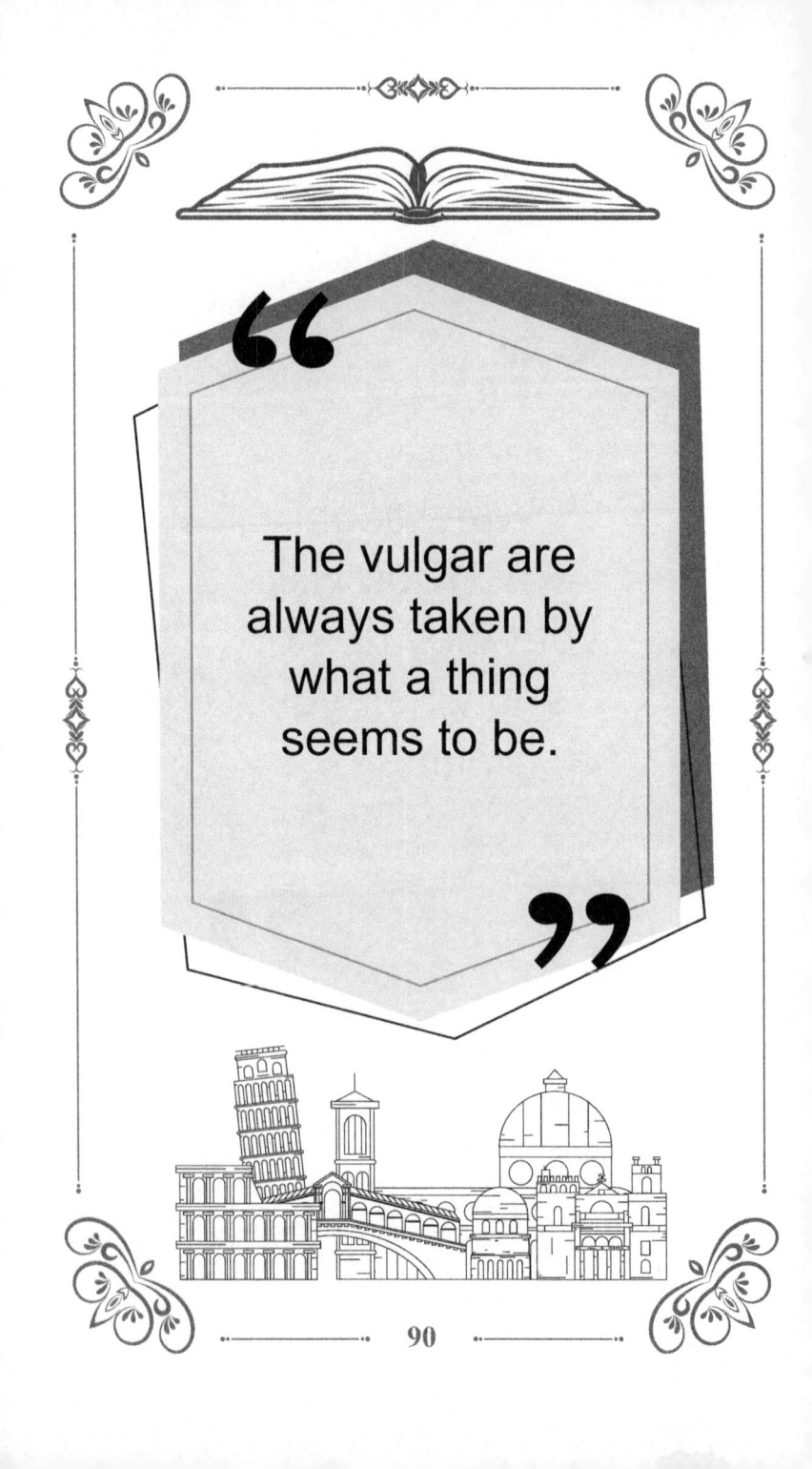

> And there is nothing wastes so rapidly as liberality, for even whilst you exercise it you lose the power to do so, and so become either poor or despised, or else, in avoiding poverty, rapacious and hated.

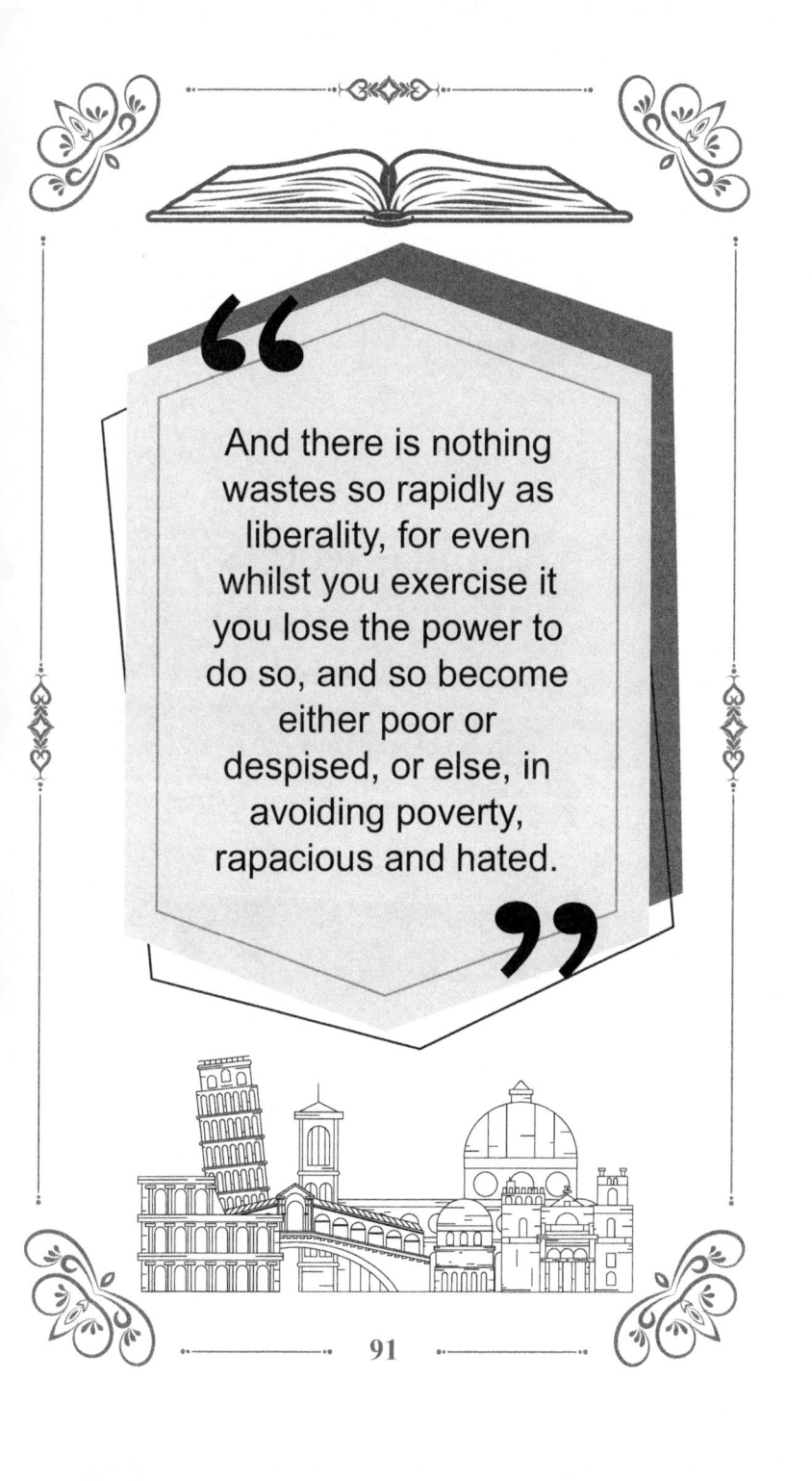

> A prince who is not wise himself will never take good advice.

> He ought to question them upon everything, and listen to their opinions, and afterwards form his own conclusions.

> You can satisfy the people, for their object is more righteous than that of the nobles, the latter wishing to oppress, while the former only desire not to be oppressed.

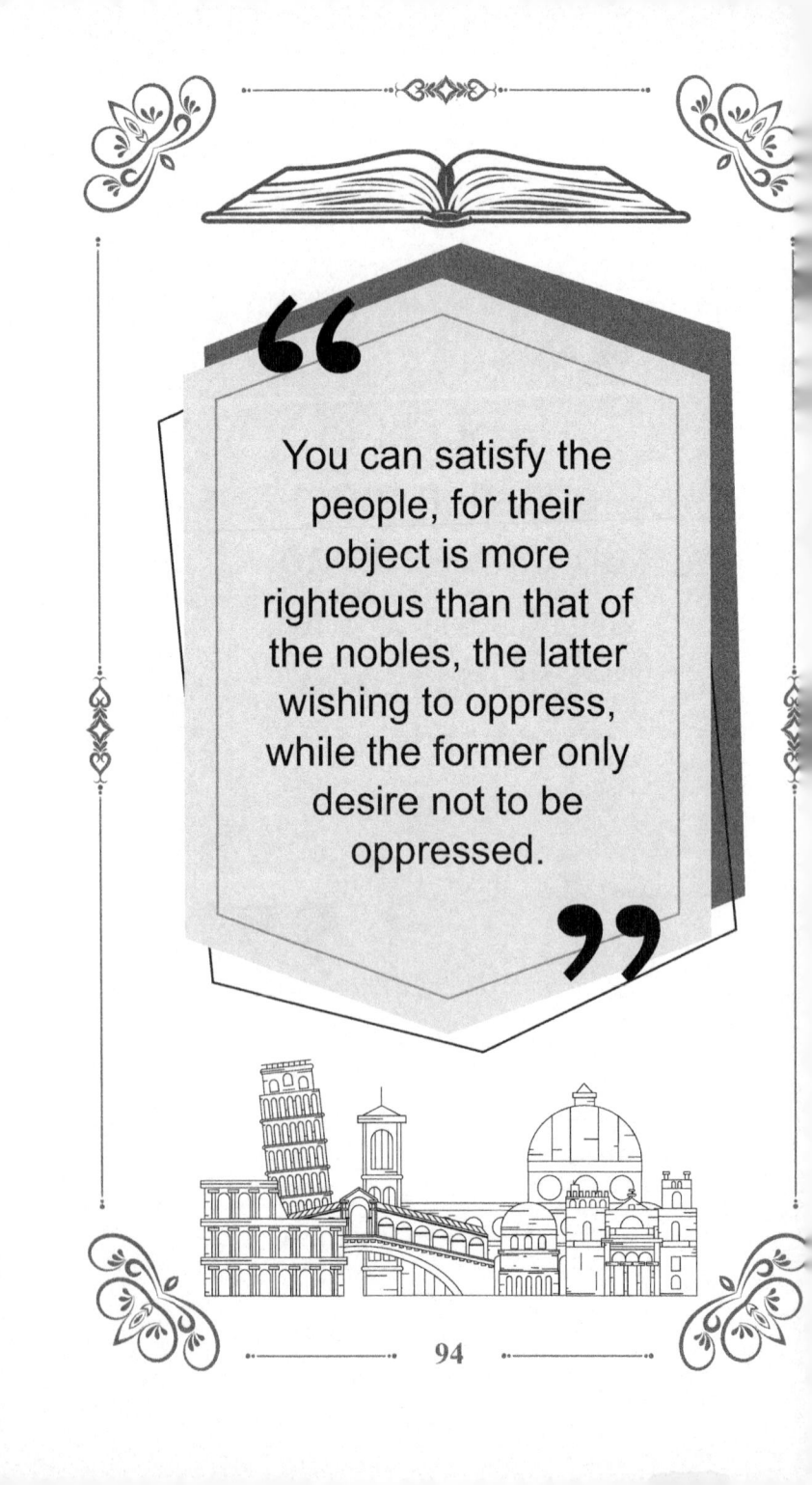

> I'm not interested in preserving the status quo; I want to overthrow it.

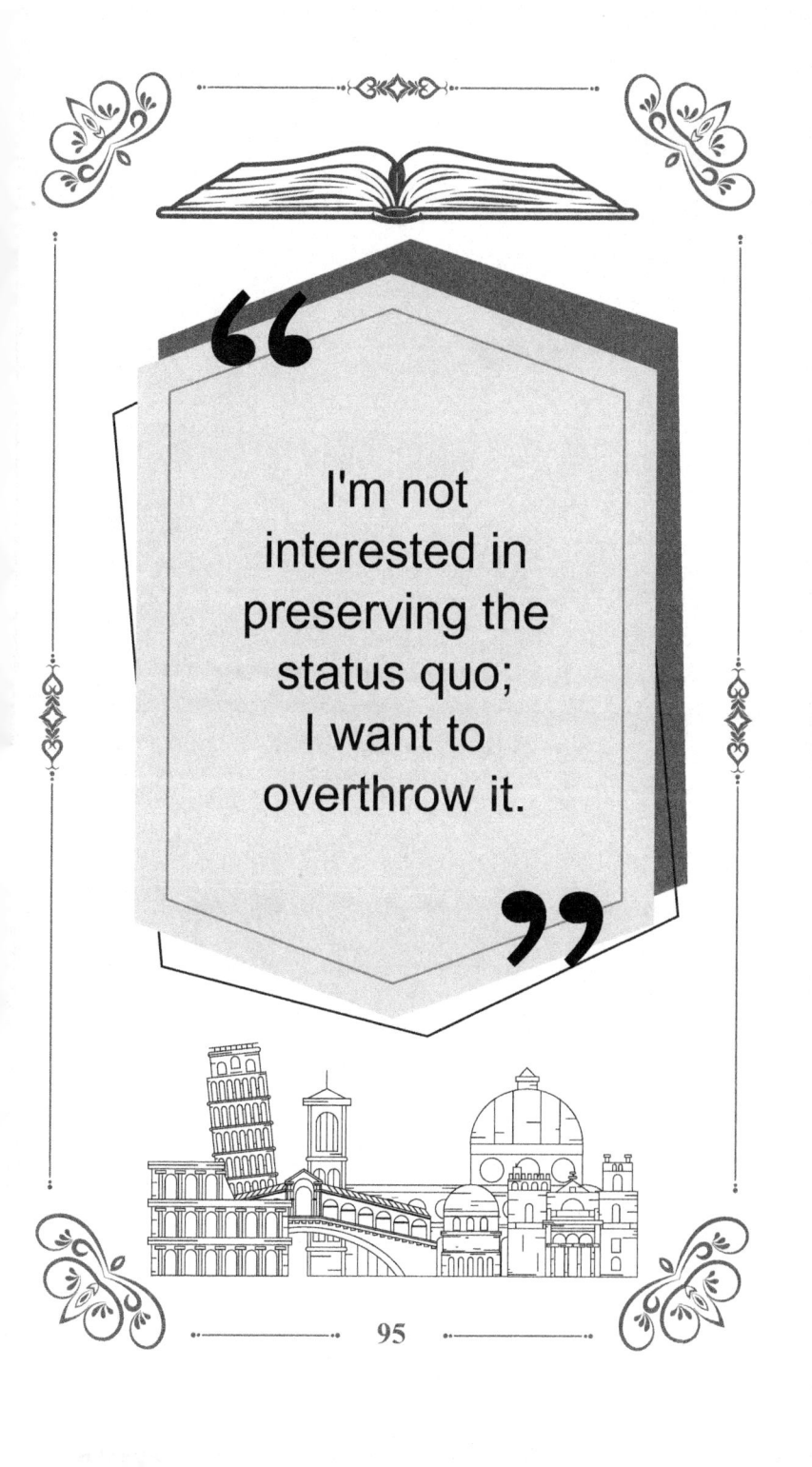

> A prince never lacks legitimate reasons to break his promise.

> It is not titles that honor men, but men that honor titles.

> Politics have no relation to morals.

> One change always leaves the way open for the establishment of others.

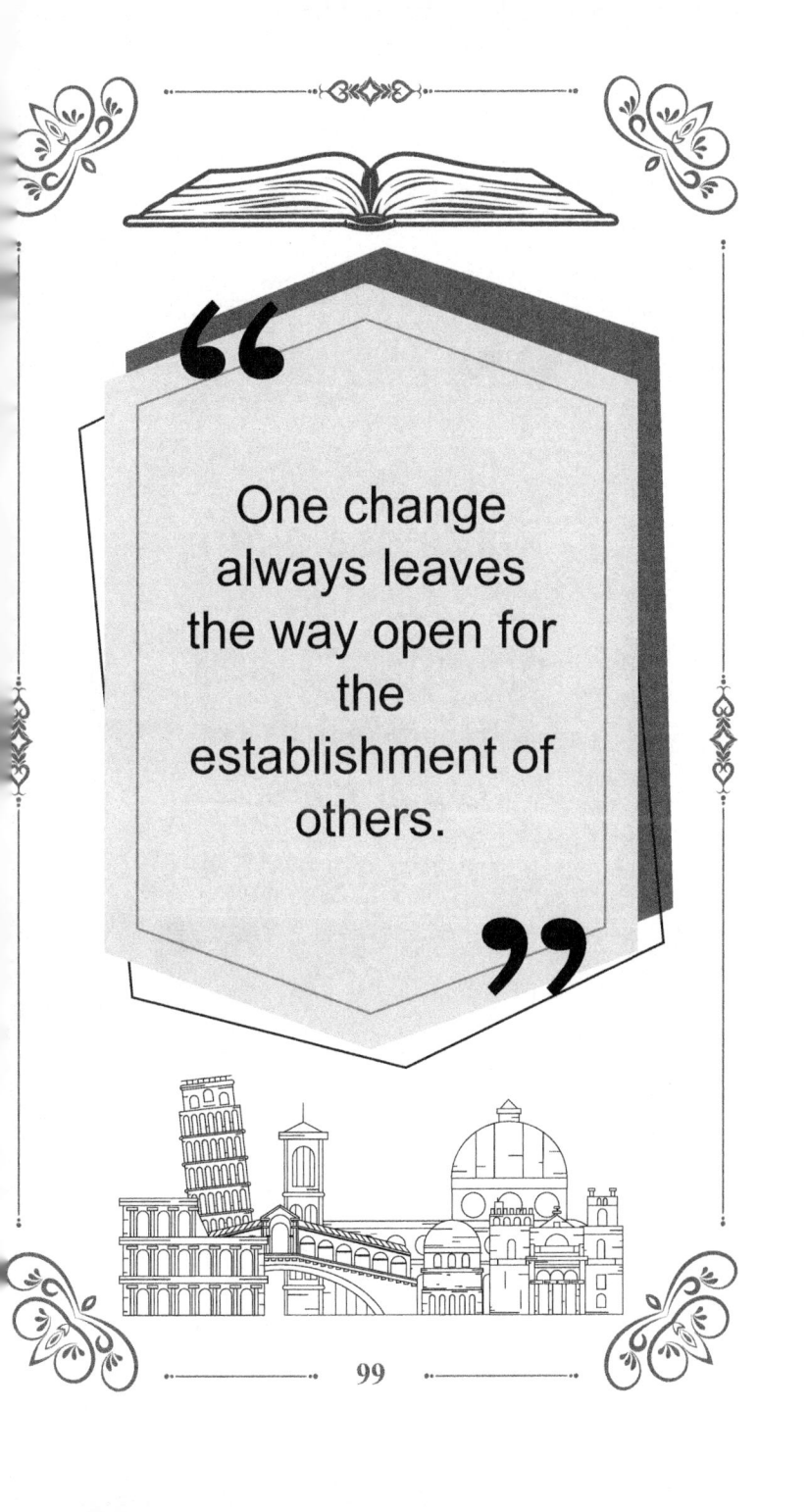

> Tardiness often robs us opportunity, and the dispatch of our forces.

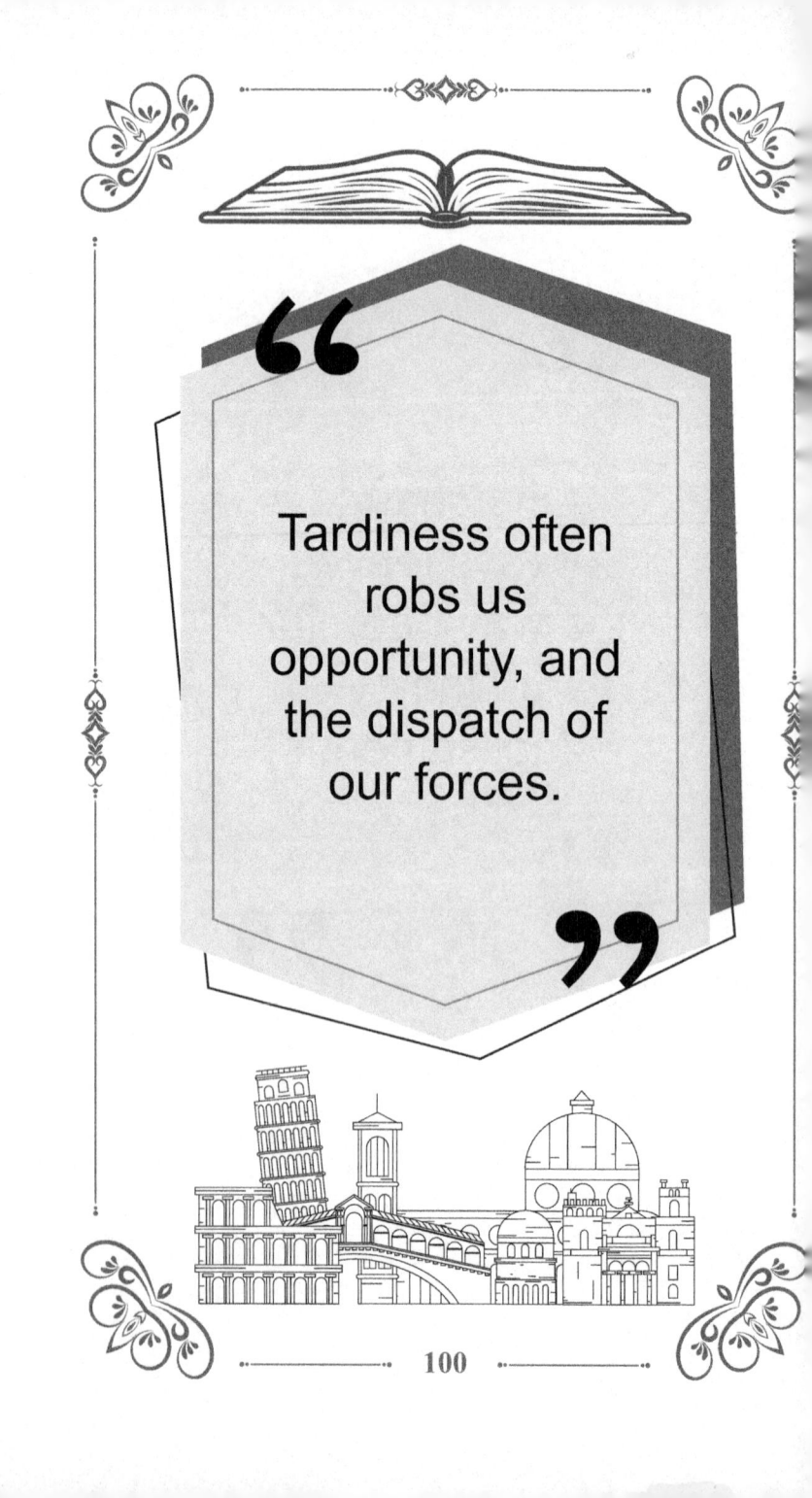

Printed in Great Britain
by Amazon